Building upon a lifetime of Bibl[...] Santo Calarco interprets the Bible as a unified narrative of creation, fall, and restoration, where the restoration he envisions includes the ultimate reconciliation of all people to God.

Now in this inspiring work, Santo Calarco articulates with conviction and considerable passion his own version of the Unconditional Love Narrative and its corollary that, according to the Bible as a whole, divine justice always expresses divine mercy and compassion.

Professor Thomas Talbott, PhD
Author of *The Inescapable Love of God*

Santo Calarco has taken the argument for universal salvation out of the realm of heresy into a new level, and must now be considered a serious theological proposition.

This biblical exegesis cannot easily be brushed off: Christians, as the noble Bereans did, will have to crack open their Bibles and see whether it is so.

Dr. Cecil Cockerham
Founder and President, American Seminary

As I was reading Santo Calarco's new book, *Amazed by Grace*, I couldn't help but visualize a cosmic Rubik's Cube being skillfully and progressively solved by its author. With each chapter, Santo deftly adjusts some part of the puzzle of Universal Restoration into greater alignment and coherence with the central truth of the universe about Jesus—He is Salvador Mundi—the Savior of the World.

Each chapter embraces a topic which heretofore might have served as an objection to Universal Restoration, but now, under Santo's rigorous and renewed exposition, each topic now tongue-and-grooves as a perfect fit with Patristic Apocatastasis —the reconciliation of all things to Christ. Judgement becomes a cleansing and curative vehicle for salvation. Justice becomes a servant vehicle of mercy, deliverance, and restoration.

The Old Testament prophets saw piecemeal parts of the puzzle in the distance. New Testament prophets saw the whole cube but it still lacked a cohesive alignment of all its conceptually colored tiles. When both eras' prophets are properly blended, Santo shows us the Rubik's Cube has been solved.

This book is not only an opus on Universal Restoration, but also an accessible primer on Apocatastasis. What's not to love?

Richard Murray
Criminal Defense Attorney
Author of *God Versus Evil, and The Jesus Mood*

Santo Calarco's obvious enthusiasm and accessible style make *Amazed by Grace* an enjoyable book to gobble up. But don't mistake his skills at teaching or his readability as an author fool you into thinking he's a theological lightweight.

Calarco is not only careful and thorough in his study of the Scriptures—he is also a prayerful and active practitioner of what he discovers. His life points us back to Christ. I have found him to be a playful provocateur and helpful interlocutor, most especially when we're not exactly on the same page. That's precisely where the treasures are found.

I commend *Amazed by Grace* as a fresh oasis to the spiritually dry and to the earnest seeker.

Brad Jersak (PhD)
St. Stephen's University, NB
Author of *A More Christlike God*

It is surely the desire of every believer that God finally save every person who ever lived. Might it be so? Universalism has long raised suspicion among evangelicals because it has seemed to minimize the centrality of Christ in salvation and the role of Scripture in defining Christian belief. Santo Calarco has minimized neither!

The one question is this: does Scripture testify that the goal of all judgment is restoration, as Santo asserts? I can think of no better statement of the case for "Yes!" than this work provides. This is a work that no evangelical believer in the alternatives of a never-ending hell or of annihilationism can ignore!

Dr. Ross Cole
Conjoint Senior Lecturer in Old Testament
Avondale College

It's not easy being a Christian. Conventional interpretations of the Word of God tell us how to behave, and what will happen if we don't. There is an implied threat—of tough love—of great reward and cruel punishment.

In *Amazed by Grace*, Dr. Calarco points out that God does not apply 'tough love' without compassion and isn't a 'quitter.' God has no intention of everlasting condemnation. There is no quitting when it comes to saving our soul.

Dr. Robert Dawson PhD
Author of *How To Be Happy In Spite Of Ourselves*

AMAZED
BY
GRACE

Unspeakable, Unstoppable, Universally
Restoring Love

SANTO CALARCO

Amazed by Grace:
Unspeakable, Unstoppable, Universally Restoring Love

Published by Loose Branch Press
San Leandro, CA | www.loosebranchpress.com

Bible translations permissions:

Unless otherwise noted, all Scripture quotations are cited from the NIV:

NIV: The Holy Bible, New International Version, NIV Copyright © 1973, 1978, 1984, 2011 by Biblica, Inc. UBP. All rights reserved worldwide.

KJV: The King James Version (Authorised): Public Domain.

NASB: The New American Standard Bible, Copyright © 1960, 1962, 1963, 1968, 1971, 1972, 1973, 1975, 1977, 1995 by the Lockman Foundation. UBP.

NKJV: The New King James Version. Copyright © 1982 by Thomas Nelson, Inc. UBP. All rights reserved.

AMP: Amplified® Bible, Copyright © 2015 by The Lockman Foundation Used by permission. www.Lockman.org

NRSV: Revised Standard Version of the Bible, Copyright © 1946, 1952, and 1971 National Council of the Churches of Christ in the United States of America. Used by permission. All rights reserved worldwide.

NLT: The Holy Bible, New Living Translation, copyright ©1996, 2004, 2015 by Tyndale House Foundation. Used by permission of Tyndale House Publishers, Inc., Carol Stream, Illinois 60188. All rights reserved.

ESV: The Holy Bible, English Standard Version, copyright © 2001 by Crossway Bibles, a publishing ministry of Good News Publishers. Used by permission. All rights reserved.

Emphases: All emphases throughout the book and the author's, including those in Scripture texts and cited material, unless otherwise indicated.

ISBN 978-1-7330931-0-1

Dedication

to Martha Sandino who provided me with the motivation, encouragement and discipline to finish this book to the best of my ability. Without her persistent nudges this work may not be in your hands today.

Foreword

by Thomas Talbott

Building upon a lifetime of Bible study, teaching, and preaching, Santo Calarco interprets the Bible as a unified narrative of creation, fall, and restoration, where the restoration he envisions includes the ultimate reconciliation of all people to God.

But the Bible is not, of course, a single text with a single (human) author; it is instead a rich and diverse set of documents that appeal to the religious imagination in a variety of complex ways. So given the diversity of interests and writing styles of its various authors, the history of some of its documents, and the variety of perspectives it includes, some scholars understandably look with suspicion upon any interpretation that would treat the entire Bible as a single unified narrative. Alternatively, some conservatives proceed almost as if a super computer with all of the relevant historical and grammatical information plugged into it could theoretically deduce a consistent and relatively complete systematic theology from the Bible as a whole. It is enough just to read the Bible as it is, they will tell you.

Both approaches to the Bible rest upon essentially the same mistake, in my opinion: the failure to appreciate the essential role of the human imagination in any coherent interpretation of the Bible as a whole. Lest some should worry about my use of the term *"human imagination"* in the present context, I would point out that this term in no way excludes a *divinely inspired* human imagination or, as a Calvinist might put it, illumination by the Holy Spirit. The point is that *any* interpretation of the Bible as a whole is as much an art and a work of the imagination, even a product of philosophical reasoning, as it is of historical and linguistic study. And that is but one reason why no amount of sophisticated Bible scholarship will ever resolve, by itself, the inconsistencies that arise between a Calvinist, an Arminian, and a universalist interpretation of the Bible as a whole. For any one of these interpretations requires that its proponents interpret some texts and some themes in light of others; it requires, as some theologians might put it, a hermeneutical principle of some kind or another. Or as some conservative Christians might say: it requires that one somehow use Scripture itself to interpret Scripture. But that, I think, is merely another way of saying that we do not read the Bible the way it is; we read it instead the way we are.

As an illustration, consider a text such as Romans 11:32 where Paul explicitly stated: "For God has imprisoned all in disobedience so that he may be merciful to all." If, like Augustine, Calvin, and other Reformed theologians, you imagine that justice and mercy are distinct (and very different) attributes of God, that God has no merciful or compassionate nature that would constrain him to forgive a single sinner, and that God therefore freely chooses to extend a special saving grace to some even as he withholds from it others, then you might very well accept Calvin's overall narrative, which includes the following interpretation of our text:

> For if they should tenaciously insist on the statement that he wills to have mercy on all, I give *by way of exception* what is written elsewhere: "Our God is in heaven where he does whatever he pleases" [Ps. 115:3]. So, then, this word is to be explained [so] as to agree with the other: "I will show mercy

to whom I will show mercy, and I will pity those whom I pity" [Ex. 33:19]. He who chooses those upon whom he is bound to show mercy *does not bestow it upon all.* But since it clearly appears that he is there concerned with classes of men, not men as individuals, away with further discussion (*Institutes,* Bk. III, Ch. XXIV, Sec. 16— my emphases).

Call this the Limited in Love and Compassion Narrative.

But if, like George MacDonald, Thomas Allin, and a number of more contemporary writers, your imagination comes to be inspired by the conviction that in God justice and mercy are the very same attribute, that even God's severity towards the disobedient and his willingness to cut them off for a season express his boundless mercy towards them, and that apart from divine forgiveness there can be no triumph of divine justice, you will likely adopt a very different narrative. Call it the Unconditional Love Narrative. Instead of concluding, as Calvin did, that the God "who chooses those upon whom he is bound to show mercy does not bestow it upon all," you will likely reason in exactly the opposite direction. Because God bestows his mercy upon all, as Romans 11:32 clearly declares, and also does whatever he pleases, as Psalm 115:3 likewise declares, it follows that to bestow mercy upon all is precisely what it pleases him to do. So yes, the one "word is to be explained [so] as to agree with the other," as Calvin insists. But from the perspective of the Unconditional Love Narrative, it will seem as if Calvin has gotten things exactly backwards. For even the declaration, "I will show mercy to whom I will show mercy, and I will pity those whom I pity" (Ex. 33:19), is arguably an idiomatic expression that expresses God's sovereign right to extend his mercy even to those, such as our own enemies, whom we humans might want to condemn. And as for Calvin's claim that in Romans 11:32 Paul had in mind classes of people rather than individuals, the parallel structure of Paul's own sentence surely belies that. Are not those *individuals* whom God has imprisoned in disobedience the *very ones,* according to this text, to whom he is merciful?

Now in this inspiring work, Santo Calarco articulates with conviction and considerable passion his own version of the Unconditional Love Narrative and its corollary that, according to the Bible as a whole, divine justice *always* expresses divine mercy and compassion. He thus points out, quite rightly in my opinion, that Romans 11:32 is not only the conclusion of Paul's discourse in Romans 9-11 concerning the problem that Israel's current unbelief posed for him; it is also the conclusion of a longer and more sustained theological argument that begins in the early chapters of Romans, where Paul first described the severe consequences of sin and God's judgment of it. "What most people [who read these early chapters] don't see," Calarco thus observes, "is the way Paul resolves the issue of sin, judgment and wrath at the end of his letter.

He says that all have sinned and as a result are exposed to judgment and wrath. But this universal sin, judgment and wrath end up in 'mercy for all'" (11:32).

Even first-rate scholars, it seems, too often fail to appreciate that you simply cannot validly infer the *absence* of a corrective purpose from harsh language alone or even from the language of retribution. For one thing, the language of correction and that of retribution are inseparably intertwined in many ordinary linguistic contexts. A man seeking pure vengeance or revenge, for example, may thus use the language of correction: "I'm going to teach him a lesson he'll never forget!" And a loving mother, seeking to correct her child forcefully, may use the language of retribution: "If you disobey me again in this matter, you will pay for it." Beyond that, none of the harsh language in the early chapters of Romans (or even in Romans 9) carries any implication of a final and irreversible rejection of those who sin in the present; hence, nothing there justifies the popular assumption that Paul did not really mean what he in fact said in 11:32. Neither does any of the harshest language anywhere else in the Bible count against Calarco's overall thesis, which he expresses in the following way: "God's justice is ultimately restorative, not retributive. When God manifests His justice and responds to evil, His goal is not to retributively damn anyone, but to restoratively heal from the inside out - as painful as this restoring process may be."

One key to an imaginative interpretation of the Bible as a whole is a willingness to remain focused on major theological themes—the big picture, so to speak—without too much distraction from the details of historical and linguistic study, as important as these are. Calarco thus writes: "As we read the big picture of the Bible and look at the forest instead of the trees, we see a clear, repeated pattern emerge. Evil is always judged, and always with a view to restoration - as painful as this process may be." So is the point in remaining focused on major theological themes that we are entitled to ignore the details of history and language whenever it suits our purpose to so? Quite the contrary. One should never ignore such details when they are truly relevant to sound exegesis. But the point, once again, is that these details almost never have a direct bearing on the disagreements that arise between Calvinists, Arminians, and universalists. For the fact is you can find first-rate Bible scholars in each of these warring camps, and it is the very nature of an inspired message, I believe, that it inevitably transcends the historical, cultural, and linguistic context in which it is initially clothed. For that reason alone, a simple farmer who is receptive to a message of love and hope might read the Bible in an English (or any other decent) translation with a lot more spiritual insight than would a sophisticated scholar who seeks to explain away Paul's explicit statement that God is merciful to all.

I predict, in any case, that Calarco may need to overcome considerable hostility from his target audience of evangelical Christians. For who can forget the hostility of that audience towards Rob Bell after the publication of his book *Love Wins?* Some of the hysterical reactions, including some public (and almost unbelievably self-righteous) calls for him to repent, demonstrated conclusively, in my opinion, that these reactions had nothing to do with careful Bible scholarship. But even Calarco's most conservative critics will likely discover that his understanding of biblical authority is no different from their own; so however much some may disagree with him theologically, no one can simply dismiss him on the ground that he fails to take Scripture seriously. Neither will it do to challenge him on some peripheral issue that has no direct bearing on his main thesis, which is this: "The Bible repeatedly presents us with the pattern of sin followed by judgment which is then followed by salvation and restoration. It is this pattern that lays the foundation for universal restoration and salvation."

I also predict that more than a few in his target audience will find Calarco's overall vision utterly compelling, provided only that they are willing to consider it carefully. For over and over again throughout the Bible we see that divine wrath and harsh judgment turns out to be, however surprisingly, an expression of mercy and a means of salvation.

Thomas Talbott -
Professor Emeritus of Philosophy, Willamette University
Author of *The Inescapable Love of God*

Table of Contents

Introduction

"Santo, you had better come to St Vincent's Hospital now. Your baby daughter Bree may die!"

"God, why?!!"

I was numb. Immediately, my heart cried out to God, "Why my innocent baby girl, God?! If you are really there, and if you are truly a good God, a God of justice, then why did you allow this to happen?!"

We have all faced crises in our lives during which we have asked a question like this—If God is good and a God of justice, then why isn't He doing more about evil in the world?

It's an age-old question that is also asked and addressed in the Bible.

> [3] *Why* do you make me look at injustice?
> *Why do you tolerate wrongdoing*?
> Destruction and violence are before me;
> there is strife, and conflict abounds.
> [4] Therefore the law is paralysed,
> and justice never prevails.

The wicked hem in the righteous,
so that *justice is perverted*. (Habakkuk 1:3-4)

When those of us in the West ask this question, we want to know *why* God allows evil in the first place. The answer we find to our question in the Bible, is not on where and how evil originated; the emphasis is on what God is doing about it. And the answers are practical, not theoretical.

So, how does God right wrongs? God's response to evil is called "justice" and His justice is intensely hands-on. God is not described as a judge that is merely sitting on a throne and making decisions. God is revealed as a judge who is actively involved in carrying out true justice: righting wrongs in a practical, effective way.

When we think of justice, we tend to think in terms of laws being upheld and people getting what they deserve when they break them. Western justice is more about retribution or payment in kind.

But the Bible shares a justice that is in contrast to our Western sense of justice. God's justice is ultimately restorative, not retributive. When God manifests His justice and responds to evil, His goal is not to retributively damn anyone, but to restoratively heal from the inside out.

> [18] Therefore the LORD waits to be *gracious* to you;
> therefore He will rise up to show *mercy* to you.
> For the LORD is a God of *justice*
> (Isaiah 30:18 NRSV)

In reading this verse, we are challenged. If God's justice manifests as grace and mercy, then perhaps God's response to evil is not intended to damn anyone as we may have thought, but rather His intention is to restore!

In this book, I intend to shed light on this restorative justice of God. You will see that when God declares war on "the nations" for their evil, God is positioning Himself to eradicate evil from *within* mankind, cleansing and restoring the peoples.

> [24] So the Lord GOD All-Powerful,
> the Mighty One of Israel, says:
> "You, *my enemies*, will not cause me any more trouble.
> *I will pay you back* for what you did.
> [25] I will turn against you
> and *clean away all your wrongs as if with soap;*
> I will take all the **worthless things** *out_of you.*
> (Isaiah 1:24-25 NCV)

Universal restoration through the eradication of evil *within* is what constitutes the justice of God. God's retribution, pay back, is about inner cleansing.

But here's the shocking twist no one saw coming. God revealed His supreme justice against evil through the Cross—and it was not retribution from God's perspective. It was not what mankind expected. Humanity commits the ultimate act of evil by crucifying the Son of God. And Luke in Acts 15 tells us God manifests His justice by reconciling the nations—in fact, the entire universe—in and through this horrific display of evil.

> [15] And you killed the Author of life, whom God raised from the dead. To this we are witnesses.

> [18] In this way God fulfilled what He had foretold through all the prophets, that His Messiah would suffer. [19] Repent therefore, and turn to God so that your sins may be wiped out, [20] so that times of refreshing may come from the presence of the Lord, and that He may send the Messiah

appointed for you, that is, Jesus,[21] who must remain in heaven until the time of ***universal restoration*** that God announced long ago through His holy prophets. (Acts 3:15, 18-21 NRSV)

Wow! Man murders Jesus, God the Son, and Father raises him from the dead. In response to this violent evil, God promises to send Jesus again so that "times of refreshing may come" which we are told is "the time of universal restoration announced long ago through His holy prophets."

The Bible describes the death and resurrection of Jesus as God's climatic response to evil which eventually results in universal restoration at the return of Jesus. This is all foretold through the Old Testament prophets.

The idea of Universal Restoration has generally been rejected and scoffed at within Christian circles. In most cases, those who advocate some kind of Christian Universalism usually rely on "proof-texting"—isolated verses from the Bible that are strung together to try and prove their case. I was unsatisfied with this approach and found it totally unconvincing. God placed the desire in my heart to present a comprehensive, robust, respectable doctrine of Universal Restoration that encompasses the broad sweep of the entire Bible. I wanted to present Universal Restoration within a larger unfolding story and context that is found throughout the Bible. In this short volume, I intend to present Universal Restoration within the framework of God's Justice and response to evil.

The central message of the Bible is this: God does respond to evil, and He does so because His justice demands it!

But what is God's justice all about and does it have any resemblance to Western justice? Just how restorative is God's justice? Does it involve damnation at all?

In most Western Christian views, God manifests His justice and responds to evil decidedly and eventually through hell; this is typically described as either eternal conscious torment or instant annihilation.

Is this what the Bible says about God's final victory over evil? I believe the Bible shows us that God's victory over evil is restoration—not damnation or annihilation! I intend to show that God's inherent justice is restorative; it's the only form of justice that deals with evil at the level of His essence and acts on it from the inside out.

In His justice, God has targeted evil; His aim is to take away "sin" as a power within, and His intention is to restore His entire groaning creation. And God does not "miss the mark."

I am going to unpack this marvellous story from Genesis to Revelation, demonstrating that God's successfully accomplished response to evil is universal restoration—not eternal conscious torment or instant annihilation.

Now that you know where I am coming from, please note the way universal restoration and God's war on evil are intertwined throughout the Bible. This one theme surfaces again and again: God declares war on evil in the nations, He "consumes" them, and somehow the nations come through this war renewed and restored.

Since God responds to evil through His justice because God is a God of justice, then we need to make sure we have a firm grip on what God's justice is really about.

Before we delve deeper into justice, let's consider what the storyline of the Bible is to see how justice and universal salvation fit into it.

Before we begin, here are some of my assumptions.

Biblical Affirmations

> *I believe that salvation is by grace alone through faith in the faithfulness of the doing and dying of Jesus.*

> *I believe that faith is not the cause of our salvation, but that it is our response to the finished work of Jesus.*

> *I believe in the need for missions as well as the preaching of justification by faith without works.*

> *I believe in repentance.*

My belief in Universal Restoration through the faithfulness of Jesus is built on a particular understanding of justice, wrath and judgment.

Let me explain.

If the traditional view of hell as eternal conscious torment without escape is true, then universal salvation or restoration in any form is impossible.

The modern idea of hell is based on the notion that God's justice for rejecting Jesus and/or continued sin is eternal punishment without end.

In this scenario, justice is based solely in terms of retributive, damning punishment.

But what if justice, judgment and wrath are solely about restoration? Then hell would have to be in alignment with what God is doing (God is not working against Himself), which would make it a place of cleansing in the presence of the restorative love and justice of God—which is exactly what I am convinced it is. This means that salvation and restoration are available beyond the grave.

So, the first chapters of this book will examine what the Bible says about judgment and justice. The way we understand these terms determines how we understand hell—since it is put in place to accomplish justice.

If hell is solely restorative, then universal restoration is the end result.

CHAPTER ONE

Origins of Universal Restoration: In the Beginning

What is the basic storyline of the Bible about? Professor N. T. Wright asserts that the Bible is not primarily about a set of beliefs about God, and that it is not even a progressive revelation about who God is; it is not telling us about God in theory. The Bible is "written to tell the story about what God has done, is doing and will do about evil … the underlying narrative logic of the whole Old Testament assumes that this is what it's about."[1]

God's justice demands that He responds to evil in a righteous manner. This idea comes into focus early on in Genesis and pivots around the call of Abraham.

The whole Old Testament hinges on one story: the call of Abraham in Genesis 12. All the chapters before it lead up to this passage, and

---

[1] N. T. Wright, "Evil and the Justice of God," 2006, pp. 45–46.

the rest of the Bible, including the New Testament, unpacks this story. How?

Genesis 1-11 speaks of beginnings. God begins by creating a perfect world with peace and harmony. Not much focus is given to describing what was happening in the world after the creation of Adam and Eve. Our attention is immediately focused on the entrance of evil: the serpent entices humanity's parents to choose independent "eating" over God's instruction as the source of knowledge and life, with death as the result. As we continue to read, we see how this evil spreads, multiplying throughout the world. Cain kills his brother. Lamech, the descendant of Cain, commits even greater evil and violence than Cain. Finally, the world is engulfed in evil:

> [5] The LORD saw how great the wickedness of *the human race had become* on the earth, and that every inclination of the thoughts of the human heart was only *evil all the time.* (Genesis 6:5)

After the flood, evil raised its ugly head again worldwide at the time of Babel where all humanity reinforces the choice of Adam and Eve to try to achieve a life independent of God—which is the root of all evil (Genesis 11:4).

It's at this point in time that we begin to see that God's judgments against evil are restorative in purpose. The story of Babel lays this foundation and becomes a model for the rest of Scripture.

Nik Ansell, professor of theology at the Institute for Christian Studies in Toronto asserts: "judgment is not an end in itself, and is therefore not 'final' in that sense, but is *always* a judgment unto salvation."[2]

---

[2] http://theotherjournal.com/2009/04/20/hell–the–nemesis–of–hope/

It is this understanding of judgment and justice against evil that calls for a re-reading of many biblical passages: God's judgments are *perceived* by humans to be retributive, but they are in fact restorative—hence the paradox in Scripture.

Divine Paradox: Judgment Unto Universal Salvation

As we consider the unfolding story in Genesis 1-11, we see a number of key themes re-emerging. The original blessing in Eden was "be fruitful, multiply and fill the earth." This was God's universal will for mankind. As we see, evil spread through the whole world which resulted in a worldwide flood. After the flood, we read the original blessing again: "So God blessed Noah and his sons and said to them: Be fruitful and multiply and fill the earth" (Genesis 9:1). **God is committed to this original universal blessing and acted to bring this blessing back on track.**

It's now that we find the first mention of "the nations" which becomes a major theme for the rest of the Bible. Noah's three sons became the fathers of all the nations of the earth as they began to "multiply and spread throughout the world" (Genesis 10:1,5,20,31-32), thus fulfilling God's will—to universally bless all nations!

But very soon, we find all mankind, the nations, in rebellion against God's will to fill the earth—part of the universal blessing. At Babel, "the *whole* earth" had formed one language and had gathered together in one place: "let us make a name for ourselves lest we be scattered abroad over the face of the whole earth" (Genesis 11:4). It is clear that they perceived being scattered over the face of the whole earth as a curse. What God meant for good, they saw as bad! God had commanded them to be fruitful, multiply and fill the entire earth. They had been living in this original universal blessing, but now they misunderstood it and came against it: they saw the blessing in terms of curse: "lest we be scattered"!

God intervenes by confusing their languages and spreading them around the earth. God's action was indeed a judgment *but only unto salvation*: God only had original universal blessing and the restoration to Eden in mind for the whole world at the time of Babel.

It is crucial to see how the judgment of Babel is not a punishment, even though mankind perceived it to be. The judgment is solely intended to be a universal blessing heading back to Eden. God's judgment is a positive action on the part of God to His commitment to His original universal blessing.

What this particular judgment reveals is this: it is futile to try and block the will of God insofar as it relates to God's original plan of universal blessing—even though is it now manifesting as judgment unto salvation. What the people at Babel saw as retribution was in fact a work towards restoration.

We need to come to grips with this dynamic; the things God does leading to restoration are sometimes understood by us as punitive retribution!

After the story of Babel, we read of the call of Abraham where God promises to bless him and "all the nations" through His Seed, which we know is Jesus (Genesis 12:3; 18:18; 26:4; Galatians 3:8,16). The seed of universal restoration is now sown and will be revealed and developed gradually throughout the Bible.

Herein lays the foundation of universal restoration. It is through this blessing that God intends to deal with the problem of evil within the nations—permanently. The pattern is now clearly set; the rest of Holy Writ unpacks this theme. The rest of Genesis to the end of Revelation shows us the way God engages evil within the nations and is committed to eradicating evil as He restores the world.

To this theme we now turn.

CHAPTER TWO

Judgment unto Salvation

"Luke, no! I told you not to do that!" My brother raised his voice as he spoke to his 4-year-old grandson. They were both in the garden shed, and Luke was reaching up, trying to get at things on the shelf. Joe had warned him a number of times that he could get hurt by doing this, as things could fall on him. As it was, the boy was able to shake the bench, and a bottle fell, shattering at his feet.

Was Joe angry? Yes he was! He was angered, but not because Luke directly went against his word. Joe was not personally grieved that his commandments had been disobeyed. Joe was angry because Luke had nearly seriously hurt himself. So he picked up his grandson and put him into time out. Warning was followed by wrath and judgment, but it was only unto salvation.

The Bible says the same thing about the wrath and judgment of God.

Consider this.

[18] They pour out drink offerings to other gods to arouse my anger. [19] But am I the one they are provoking? declares the LORD. Are they not rather *harming themselves*, to their own shame? (Jeremiah 7:18-19)

Yes, God is angered by our sin, and wrath and judgment do follow. But it is never because God has some pent up emotions that He has to release. God's wrath and judgment come as a result of our own self-harm, and they are released only with good intentions in mind.

We have been conditioned to think of doom and gloom when we hear the word "judgment." We tend to think that it is only or mainly about punishment or damnation. But this is not the case in the Bible. To be sure, judgment can be painful to us: discipline indeed can hurt, but the goal of proper discipline is never to harm; it is to put one back on track to wholeness.

Judgment is about discipline:

> [32] Nevertheless, when we are judged in this way by the Lord, we are being disciplined (1 Corinthians 11:32)

Discipline can be painful but fruitful:

> [11] No discipline seems pleasant at the time, but painful. Later on, however, it produces a harvest of righteousness and peace for those who have been trained by it (Hebrews 12:11)

In the previous chapter, we saw that Genesis introduces a key principle that the rest of the Bible develops: God will judge evil within nations to work towards His intention/His plan. Judgment is not the final word, either. It is not an end in itself, but a means to an end. Mercy triumphs over judgment.

Let's look at this dynamic further.

As we read the big picture of the Bible and look at the forest instead of the trees, we see a clear, repeated pattern emerge. Evil is always judged, and always with a view to restoration—as painful as this process may be.

Western Christianity has conditioned most of us to think of eternal damnation when we read about the final judgment in the Bible. This is because of the assumptions many make about the text. But judgment at the end of time is simply a culmination of judgment that has taken place throughout all time. It is only as we learn what the whole Bible says about judgment that we can truly begin to understand what the final judgment is really about. The final judgment is only a culmination in nature and purpose of all previous judgments!

The Bible speaks on this with one voice: judgment is unto salvation, not damnation. Judgment does not close the door to salvation. To the contrary, judgment is about bringing all to repentance so that they walk through the gate to salvation and restoration.

Let's quickly go through scripture and look at this pattern. Afterwards, I will slow down the pace and look at some of the individual trees in more detail.

Sin, Judgment, Salvation

Salvation follows judgment in the Bible. The Bible repeatedly presents us with the pattern of sin followed by judgment which is then followed by salvation and restoration. It is this pattern that lays the foundation for universal restoration and salvation.

God frequently had the prophets warn Israel to turn from their sinful ways and repent. The prophets often describe Israel as an adulterous wife or a rebellious son.

Consider The Prophet Hosea

When Israel abandons God, we read that God responds in anger and cries out in pain in terms of a betrayed husband: "You have abandoned me and gone after other gods. I am not your husband. Let her remove the adulterous look from her face and the unfaithfulness from between her breasts" (Hosea 2:1-2). Judgment and wrath follow: "I will punish her for the days she burned incense to the Baals [gods] because she forgot me" (Hosea 2:13). Can you hear the unrequited love in the broken heart of the heavenly Lover? Can you feel the passion and the pain as He says "she forgot me"? Yes, judgment follows sin.

Let me make a point here. Many modern translations insert the word "punish" in this verse. The Hebrew word actually means "to visit."

Note how the Amplified Bible correctly renders the original language:

> [13] And I will visit [punishment] upon her for the feast days of the Baals (Hosea 2:13 AMP)

When the Amplified Bible places words in brackets it is providing us with interpretations of words alongside the literal translations. The Hebrew says that God "visits" Israel for abandoning Him. Now this visit is not a walk in the park, but to insert the word punishment is translator bias, and in Western Christianity, this word comes with a lot of unbiblical baggage. No doubt some kind of disciplinary action is intended here, but as we shall see, the intention and outcome is purely restorative. God wants His bride back.

Eventually God says, "you will call Me 'my husband' … I will betroth you to Me forever" (Hosea 2:16,19).

Sin is followed by judgment which is solely unto salvation and restoration. God wants His marriage restored, and judgment can be part of this painful, restorative process. Did you see what Father said? "I will betroth you to Me"! Don't we normally betroth ourselves to others? But in this case, Father takes it upon Himself to make our vows to Him on our behalf. And this promise will last forever! Now this is passion!

This is just so important that I would like to repeat this point: In Western Christianity, "judgment" is usually thought of in terms of a retribution which closes down salvation; this is not the biblical picture at all, and so we need to carefully define our terms by how they are used in the Bible. In the Bible, judgment results in salvation. And because of this, we really need to reread the judgment passages in the Old Testament and note this dynamic at work. Here are some more examples.

Ezekiel also speaks of God's relationship with His people as a marriage.

Judgment Unto Salvation In Ezekiel

God says of Israel's betraying sin, "You adulterous wife! You prefer strangers instead of your own husband!" (Ezekiel 16:32) Eventually God's wrath and judgment are released. Notice the form in which they manifest.

> [26] You engaged in prostitution with the Egyptians, your neighbors with large genitals, and *aroused my anger* with your increasing promiscuity. [27] *So I stretched out my hand* against you and reduced your territory; *I gave you over to* the greed of *your enemies*, (Ezekiel 16:26-27)

Israel cheats on their heavenly Husband. God warns and calls them back over a long period of time. But yearning turns to wrath. Judgment falls. But notice that God didn't actively do anything.

Judgment and wrath simply means that God lets go. He hands people over to their lovers fully knowing that harm will come. Judgment and wrath are passive acts of God. They experience punishment from their other lovers!

> [39] Then *I will deliver you into the hands of your lovers*, and *they will tear down* your mounds *and destroy* your lofty shrines. *They will strip you* of your clothes and take your fine jewelry and leave you stark naked. (Ezekiel 16:39)

Here it is again: the wrath of God is clearly a *figure of speech* that simply means He lets go and allows consequences to follow unhindered. It is the lovers that destroy and strip—not God!

Let's examine the ancient way of thinking on this. In Old Testament times, it was believed that what God allows, He does!

God's wrath is passive, indirect and consequential. But since God is the original cause of everything as the supreme Creator, in a sense, the buck stops with Him. To the Old Testament believer this meant that everything was under God's control—even the negative circumstances were considered acts of divine wrath—albeit passive on God's side!

This is a huge insight that we will come across again and again in the Bible. Paul says the same thing in Romans 1:18, 24, 26, 28. Paul says that in His wrath against the sin of idolatry, God hands people over to their choices and allows them to experience the consequences their idolatrous choices create. He calls this the wrath of God and also later tells us that this wrath is restorative in intent and outcome. We will look closer at that when we reach the New Testament.

So far, Ezekiel has spoken of sin, wrath and judgment. Look what follows.

⁵³ "'However, *I will restore* the fortunes of *Sodom* and her daughters and of Samaria and her daughters, *and your* fortunes along *with them* …

⁵⁵ And your sisters, *Sodom* with her daughters and Samaria with her daughters, *will return* to what they were before; *and you* and your daughters *will return* to what you were before. (Ezekiel 16:53, 55)

So there you have it! Sin followed by wrath and judgment are ultimately followed by restoration! Oops! It says here Sodom will be restored too. But doesn't the Bible say that Sodom experienced the punishment of eternal fire in Jude 7? Yes indeed! So if they will be restored, then this means that eternal fire was not their end—it is not all over for them. Many of us in the West have totally misunderstood what punishment by eternal fire really means! We have misunderstood both judgment and eternal fire. More on this later.

The pattern of sin, judgment and salvation-restoration repeats itself over and over again in the Old Testament.

Other prophets speak of God's relationship with Israel as Father-child instead of as Husband-Wife.

Let's consider this.

God says to the people of Israel, "I reared children and brought them up, but they have rebelled against Me" (Isaiah 1:2). They were utterly estranged from their Father (Isaiah 1:4). Wrath and judgment came as a result from the hands of their enemies (Isaiah 1:7). But it didn't end there.

These self-induced consequences were only temporary and were allowed only to bring His children back home. Later, God says:

^{24}"Ah! I will vent my wrath on my foes
and avenge myself on my enemies.
^{25} I will turn my hand against you;
I will thoroughly purge away your dross
and remove all your impurities.
^{26} I will restore your leaders as in days of old,
your rulers as at the beginning.
Afterward you will be called
the City of Righteousness,
the Faithful City." (Isaiah 1:24-26)

Wow! This is pretty graphic language and is a clear metaphor. Isaiah speaks of wrath and judgment in terms of *smelting*. God will purge away dross and remove impurities from the gold for the purpose of refining. In so doing, He is restoring!

Note two important things here. The text is indented as poetry, so it is not narrative or prose. When we encounter poetry, we are to expect poetic speech. Poetry lends itself to emotion, drama, hyperbole and exaggeration for the sake of emphasis! Metaphors abound and are blended. And that's exactly what we find here.

God vents His wrath, described metaphorically as placing His children in smelting fires to clear away the dross in order to refine and restore. Did you notice that this is how God gets revenge? He says "I will avenge myself" as He reacts to their sin. But God gets His revenge by purifying and restoring His kids! I just wrote myself happy! Remember that this is poetry filled with vivid images.

Retributive language is symbolically speaking of a restorative outcome. Now, this is a huge truth that will help you understand all the blood and guts we read in the Bible. Retributive aggressive language is used to describe passion and pain on the part of the one hurt; but it is used only as a poetic literary device to passionately display the driving force behind ultimate restoration.

Isaiah uses this pattern quite a lot.

Before we consider some more examples from Isaiah, I want to connect all of this with theodicy. Theodicy tries to explain the following: If God is good and just, then what is He doing about evil?

The Bible answers this question as I have already pointed out, but it does not answer it in a way that satisfies our Western mindset, does it? Instead of speaking about why God allowed evil in the first place, the Bible speaks more about what God is doing and will continue to do about it, and this involves a lot of "letting it happen for a time."

The book of Genesis begins with the entrance of evil into God's good creation. But we are not told why God allows evil to enter human history in the form of a serpent. The focus is more on what God's just response to evil is. We read in aggressive violent language that God will "crush" the serpent's head through the "seed" of the woman! And by mentioning the word "seed" here, Moses has introduced us to the central theme of the entire Bible. We have seen that it would be through the "seed" of Abraham that God would bless all nations, and the apostles made it clear that the "Seed" is indeed Jesus who crushes Satan's head on the cross (John 12:31; Colossians 2:15; Hebrews 2:14-15).

Right from the beginning of the Bible, we read about God's just response to evil in violent, "crushing," warlike language. This theme is the very theme of the entire Bible and lays the foundation for all the violent language attributed to God, including the book of Revelation. We know this language is all clearly metaphor because we read that the climax of this "warfare" took place when Jesus offered himself as a passive, non-aggressive lamb on the cross. It was as a passive Lamb that Jesus prevailed over evil and won the war (Revelation 5:5-9).

The Bible doesn't tell us why God allowed evil to exist in the first place. It tells us that God doesn't immediately eliminate it, that He allows it to exist, that He contains it from getting totally out of control, and most importantly, that He works from within it to heal the whole of mankind!

N.T. Wright:

> "Somehow, strangely (and to us sometimes even annoyingly), the Creator God will not simply abolish evil from His world. The question that swirls around these discussions is, Why not? We are not given an answer; we are instead informed in no uncertain terms that God will *contain* evil, that He will *restrain* it, that He will prevent it from doing its worst, and that He will even on occasion use the malice of human beings to further His own strange purposes."[3]

Wright goes on to point out that God will work from within evil to bring about His purposes. Agreed. But I want to point out that universal restoration is the final goal. God has made a good creation that needs rescuing and liberation (Romans 8:20-22). God engages evil within creation only to rescue and restore the creation! God's war on evil results in universal restoration.

As we travel through the Bible we encounter a repeated dynamic. In many of the passages where we read that God declares war on the nations, we see that after God's wrath, anger and fire have been poured out onto the nations, that the nations end up being restored as a result! This pattern in the Old Testament comes to a climax in the book of Revelation, which we will also examine in due course.

---

[3] Wright, Evil and the Justice of God, p. 55

Let me state this again: we will find many violent, war-like images in the Bible. They seem to speak of one thing: God has declared war on evil and He is dealing with it. This language itself is violent and aggressive. But this language is clearly metaphor. The Bible repeatedly uses these images to make the point that God is indeed taking action against evil with a vengeance and with a restorative end in mind.

This means that we are not supposed to take the violent language literally—as if God is literally wiping out the nations. The language fits the theme: God has declared *war* against evil, and this idea is correctly conveyed in aggressive language and images. Evil exists within man, and God is dedicated to its eradication in order to restore humanity.

This means that as we travel through the Bible, we will see this violent language appears repeatedly. View it for what it is and how it is intended to be taken—metaphor for the sake of emphasis. It speaks of one thing: God is involved in humanity, and He has taken aggressive steps to rescue mankind from the grip of evil.

This point will become clearer as we travel through the Bible.

Let's stick with Isaiah for now.

Isaiah not only speaks of Israel's judgment unto salvation, but he says the exact same thing of all the nations. God has decreed judgment on all the nations:

> [1] Come near, *you nations*, and listen;
> pay attention, you peoples!
> Let *the earth* hear, and *all that is in it,*
> *the world*, and all that comes out of it!
> [2] The LORD *is angry with all nations;*
> his *wrath is on all their armies.*

> He will totally destroy them,
> he will give them over to slaughter. (Isaiah 34:1-2)

Here we have a clear example of military language. God intends to release His wrath against all the armies of the world. Is this language meant to be taken literally, or is it metaphor? What specifically about them ends up getting slaughtered?

Well, in contrast the same book tells us that God intends to save all the nations of the earth.

> [22] "Turn to me and *be saved*,
> all you *ends of the earth*;
> for I am God, and there is no other.
> [23] By myself I have sworn,
> my mouth has uttered in all integrity
> a word that will not be revoked:
> Before me *every knee will bow*;
> by me every tongue will swear.
> [24] *They will say* of me, '*In the* LORD *alone*
> *are deliverance* and strength.'"
> *All who have raged against him*
> *will come to him* and be put to shame. (Isaiah 45:22-24)

Oh my goodness!

On the one hand it looks like the world is going to be exterminated under the military hand of God, and yet we also read that every single knee that was at one time raging against God will bow in salvation and declare that in God alone is deliverance!

I deal with this passage and Isaiah 19 in greater detail later on in the book where I examine the book of Isaiah.

Consider one more example from Isaiah in point form.

Sin: The people worship other gods and the true God is jealous (Isaiah 57:6, 9–11).

Judgment: God intervenes through wrath by hiding His face!

[17] I was *enraged* by their sinful greed;
I punished them and *hid my face in anger*,
yet they kept on in their wilful ways. (Isaiah 57:17)

Did you see that one? God's judgment/punishment manifested in His wrath by *hiding His face*! Wow! Many of us really had this all wrong, didn't we? God's wrath is passive here too. God lets people go and do what they want and experience the self-generated consequences with the intent to bring them to salvation.

Salvation–Restoration:

[18] I have seen their ways, *but I will heal* them;
I will guide them *and restore* comfort to Israel's mourners,
[19] *creating praise* on their lips.
Peace, peace, to those far and near,"
says the LORD. "And *I will heal them*." (Isaiah 57:18–19)

Once again we see the same pattern emerge: sin of idolatry leading to judgment which leads to restoration and healing!

Judgment is not the last word; healing and restoration are. Judgment is always unto salvation.

This point is the underlying issue of this book. It is so important that we understand that judgment is unto salvation that I want you to see how it is deeply ingrained in many of the major prophets and their messages.

Judgment Unto Salvation of the Nations In Amos

> [7] "Are not you **Israelites**
> **the same to me as the Cushites?"**
> declares the LORD.
> "Did I not **bring Israel up from Egypt**,
> the **Philistines from Caphtor**
> and the **Arameans from Kir**? (Amos 9:7–12)

Here's a question: where do we get the idea that God was exclusive in the Old Testament? Nationalism seems to be crumbling as far as Amos is concerned! When we read the phrase "Did I not bring out Israel from the land of Egypt," we are reading the about the very epicentre of covenant! I really don't know how else to say this—Amos is saying that God had covenant–relationships with all nations in Old Testament times. Of course, Israel had a special role, but this didn't mean that God had abandoned the rest of the world. God clearly entered into redeeming relationships with other nations in Old Testament times.

Universalism seems to be flourishing in the prophets. And yet for all this, it was going to be through the Seed of Abraham (Jesus) that all of this would be pulled in together. More on this later.

For now, Amos provides us with a strong clue.

> [11] "In that day
> "**I will restore** David's fallen shelter—
> I will repair its broken walls
> and **restore** its ruins—
> and will rebuild it as it used to be,

^{12} **so that they may possess** the remnant of **Edom
and** *all* **the nations** that bear my name,"
declares the LORD, who will do these things.
(Amos 9:11–12)

"In that day"? Which day? This phrase is used repeatedly to refer to the time of the Messiah when the New Covenant would be ratified—a new covenant that was going to be universal and with all people. Amos is saying that David's restored shelter would reach out to "all the nations that bear My name." Jesus called the Twelve together as the judges of Israel, and he told them to go and preach the Gospel of the New Covenant to all nations—Remember? Oops, getting ahead of myself again.

Amos is telling us that when David's shelter is restored that all the nations would seek God. The New Testament, when James quotes this passage: "God first visited the Gentiles (nations), to take out of them a people for His name" so that all nations, all the rest of mankind would end up seeking God (Acts 15:14–18). As a result we are told that all the nations would be gathered as one people universally united.

Judgment Unto Salvation in Jeremiah

The prophet Jeremiah reveals this same pattern a number of times with reference to particular nations.

MOAB:

> **Sin:** Moab to be punished and to remain desolate–Jeremiah 48:4,9

> **Judgment:** Moab will be destroyed–Jeremiah 48:42

Restoration: After the judgment comes restoration–Jeremiah 48:47

AMMON:

Sin and Judgment: Will be judged by fire–Jeremiah 49:1,2

Restoration: After the judgment of fire comes restoration– Jeremiah 49:6

ELAM:

Sin and Judgment: They sin, judgment will make an "end" of them– Jeremiah 49:37–38

Restoration: "Behold I will restore" after He has made an "end of them"! "Making an end of them" obviously doesn't mean what we would tend to think– Jeremiah 49:39

Judgment Unto Salvation in Malachi

Again. I will lay it down in point form for your personal study.

Sin: People calling evil good–Malachi 2:17–3:1

Judgment: Takes the form of "fire"–Malachi 3:2

Salvation–restoration: The fiery judgment is likened to soap that refines, cleanses and restores Malachi 3:2–4.

Now, let's closely examine this theme in one of the most graphic books in the Bible.

Judgment unto Salvation in Zephaniah

The theme of this book is the day of the Lord when God's wrath is poured out onto all the nations. First we read of the sin and God's universal reaction to sin and evil.

> [14] The **great day of the LORD** is near—
> near and coming quickly.
> The cry on the day of the LORD is bitter;
> **the Mighty Warrior shouts His battle cry.**
> [15] That day will be **a day of wrath**—
> a day of **distress and anguish,**
> a day of trouble and ruin,
> a day of darkness and gloom,
> a day of clouds and blackness—
> [16] a day of trumpet and **battle cry**
> **against the fortified cities**
> and against the corner towers.
>
> [17] "I will bring such distress on all people
> that they will grope about like those who are blind,
> because they have sinned against the LORD.
> **Their blood will be poured out like dust**
> **and their entrails like dung.**
> [18] Neither their silver nor their gold
> will be able to save them
> on the day of the LORD's wrath."
>
> In **the fire of His jealousy**
> the **whole earth will be consumed,**
> for He will **make a sudden end**
> **of all who live on the earth.** (Zephaniah 1:14–18)

Did I mention it was graphic? Let's break this passage down.

The passage is introduced in military, violent terms: God is the "Mighty Warrior" declaring His war on evil. Remember that this is simply an outworking of what we read in Genesis: God declared war on evil by promising that the serpent's head would be crushed!

We read of the universal destruction of mankind: "make a sudden end of all who live on the earth." We also see a lot of violent language: "Their blood will be poured out like dust and their entrails like dung." However, when we read about the execution of this threat in Chapter Three, we see that this language is not meant to be taken literally.

For example, did you notice that even in this chapter, God's wrath is likened to fire? And do you see that this wrath is "the fire of His jealousy"? Bingo! What we have here is a clear case of poetic metaphor. Even the translators realized this and indented the language in this chapter in poetic form instead of narrative.

So wrath and fire refer to God's jealousy. The world and all its nations belong to Him, and He will not share the world with other gods; in His fiery jealousy, God is angry, and He will not let the world go. I agree that the passage here seems to look like total annihilation of mankind. But we see in Chapter 3 that when God finally releases this fiery, wrathful jealousy—that the nations are still very much alive after the event!

This gathering of all nations for judgment is taken up again and the judgment executed in Chapter Three.

> [8] "Therefore wait for Me," says the LORD,
> "Until the day I rise up for plunder;
> My determination is to *gather the nations*
> To My assembly of kingdoms,
>
> *To pour on them* My indignation,
> *All My fierce anger*;

> *All the earth shall be devoured*
> With the *fire of My jealousy*.
> ⁹ *"For then I will restore* to the peoples a pure language,
> *That they all may call* on the name of the LORD,
> *To serve Him* with one accord. (Zephaniah 3:8–9 NKJV)

Again we read of the gathering of all nations for judgment, and again wrath and fire are used as descriptions of His jealousy.

But we encounter something strange. After God releases His wrath and fire [His jealousy], after "all the earth" is devoured we see that "then I will restore" the peoples! What?! Yes! "For then" tells us what the purpose of this fiery universal judgment was all about. The people come through this wrath of God very much alive—restored—even though they were consumed!

You see, the nations are not committed to God. But God is jealous and won't let them go. So He places them through His final judgment in order to cleanse and restore them so that they will all eventually call on His name and serve Him. Universal judgment and fire results in universal salvation and restoration!

What glory of glories! They enter the final judgment as unbelievers and exit it as restored believers all worshiping the one true God in unity. Can it be any clearer than this? The purpose of the final judgment is to deal with the sin of unbelief.

I believe that we have just read the Bible's description of hell! We have just read of the nations going through the fire of their final judgment. Were you shocked by the result? I know I was and still am shocked and amazed. Judgment results in the fire we call hell that leads to restoration and universal worship! Universal judgment leads to universal restoration and worship. Oh how I pray you get this revelation in your heart!

Judgment is only unto salvation. Father will do whatever it takes.

I want to now bring the first and last chapters of Zephaniah together.

In Zephaniah One, we read that God was the "Mighty Warrior" who set out to make war with the nations, and we saw that the war of the "Mighty Warrior" resulted in universal restoration.

But later on, we read of the "Mighty Warrior" again, after the final war on evil is over and after the nations of the world have been restored.

> [17] The LORD your God is with you,
> **the Mighty Warrior who saves**.
> He will take great delight in you;
> *in His love He* will no longer rebuke you,
> but will **rejoice over you with singing** (Zephaniah 3:17)

Can it be true? The Mighty Warrior who sets out to make war with the nations is a Mighty Warrior who restores all nations through judgement—the Mighty Warrior who saves! Yes! Judgment is unto salvation! It is "in His love" that the Mighty Warrior declares His jealous love with His sole intent to save.

Let's get past the violent language. See it for what it is. It is poetic exaggeration to describe the intense passionate love of God for all of us. I am Italian, and I can relate to this language. I love it!

The Mighty Warrior, who declares His jealous anger on the nations of the world, declares a war of love and wins it! This Love is for the whole of humanity.

What's the last scene as far as Zephaniah is concerned?

The same "Mighty Warrior" who declared war on the nations and after restoring and saving them to Himself, will "rejoice over you with singing"! I have yet again written myself happy!

What an intimate Father?! What a passionate God! Words fail me. I can't explain exactly what all of this means to me.

The Bible is a love story. Things are created good and perfect. Father comes down to the garden in the cool of every evening to talk to His kids, beautiful beings made in His image. But someone else comes between them. The Bible doesn't tell us why this happens. We are only told that it happened and that Father declares a passionate war with evil! All the language speaking of jealousy is used to describe what's going on in Father's heart. Of course it is metaphor. Of course human emotions are used to describe Father and what happens. How else can we relate to our Father unless passionate language is used?! I get it! I hope you get it too.

Father has the last word. Even though evil spreads and grows, Father's Mighty Warrior love will always prevail. Eventually, He will take up the whole world into His arms and sing and rejoice over them.

I feel like I have just finished my book. But there is so much more. We have only just begun.

Let's finish this chapter on "Judgment unto Salvation" with Solomon.

> ⁶ Place me like a seal over your heart,
> like a seal on your arm;
> *for love* is as strong as death,
> *its jealousy* unyielding as the grave.
> It *burns like blazing fire,*
> *like a mighty flame*.
> ⁷ Many waters *cannot quench* love; (Song of Songs 8:6–7)

Wrath and judgment are expressions of God's possessive, jealous love. It is so passionate that it is often expressed using violent language and imagery! Fire is a symbol of the unyielding jealousy of God that refuses to give up on those He desires; a fiery love that cannot be quenched.

Resisting this fiery passion and taking up with other lovers will feel like hell—because of what these other lovers do to you! Before we go over into the New Testament, we still have a lot to learn from the Old Testament.

We just saw how judgment leads to salvation. But why? Undergirding God's judgment is His justice. Judgment is a manifestation of the justice of God.

So exactly why does God's justice result in salvation and not damnation?

What exactly is justice? Isn't justice about people getting what they deserve?

CHAPTER THREE

God's Justice: Setting Things Right!

I went away with Tony for a three day trip into the Australian bush. Tony is a mechanical engineer. Every two weeks he would set out on a trip to monitor petrol pumps to ensure the metres were working correctly. Tony was referred to as a "justifier." He would test the metres to ensure they were "just" and if they were not he would have to "justify" them. That is, he would need to restore them to proper working order; set them right!

What does this have to do with universal restoration? Heaps!

I believe in universal restoration because of the very fabric of divine justice. God's justice is all about restoring things to proper working order; it can do nothing else. This means that when God deals with sin, the ultimate result is healing; not never–ending torment or instant annihilation.

This issue undergirds what judgment is about.

In the last chapter, we saw many examples of God's judgment leading to salvation. Undergirding God's judgment is His justice. Judgment is a manifestation of the justice of God.

This chapter is the most important part of this book in many respects. If justice is about restoration, then it is assured that all will be restored!

I will spend considerable time in this chapter exploring in detail what the justice of God is really about.

Sadly, many conceive God's justice in terms of retribution: people getting what they deserve. This perception is that if people reject Jesus, then justice demands that they get a harsh punishment for doing so. But what if justice is about healing and restoration and not about God getting even with people?

In this chapter I will show that God's justice demands the ultimate restoration of people to proper working order. In fact the root word translated "just" or "righteous" actually means to be in correct working order.

> ³⁶ You shall have *just* balances, *just* weights
> (Leviticus 19:36 NASB)

The Hebrew word translated "just" is *sadaq*. This is the word the Old Testament uses again and again when describing God! We can see from this statement that the word "just" means to have scales that are in proper working order! Can you see my point? Since God is just and righteous (same Hebrew word), His judgments accordingly set out to make things right by restoring them to proper working order! God's justice fixes what is broken; it doesn't discard it or torment it endlessly! Nothing gets fixed that way.

Justice by definition and usage in the Bible is restorative. This is why we read so many passages about God's just judgments resulting in people being restored, purified and cleansed!

God's justice seeks to fix the broken scales. So when we read that God is just, what this means is that God is about proper working order! When He sees injustice (things not working in proper order), God's wrath and judgment set out to fix that! My point is this: annihilation or endless torture never fixes what is broken and therefore are actually in contradiction to God's justice and judgment.

By nature, God's justice fixes things, nothing else. Since hell is about God's justice, then hell can only have a restorative purpose. I will demonstrate this very assertion later on.

I need to explain an interesting dynamic happening in the English language. The one Hebrew word *sadaq* can be translated either as "just" or "righteous." We have two English words that can translate the one Hebrew word. We have the same thing in Greek. The one Greek word *"dikaios"* can also be translated "just" or "righteous."[4] "So what? "you may be thinking.

These two English words seem to carry different meanings. We have the same thing happening with the words "justice" and "righteousness." In English, we can translate the Greek word *dikaiosune* **either** as justice, **or** as righteousness. This means that when the New Testament talks about the "righteousness of God" (which for Paul is what the Gospel is that saves!!!), what we are reading about is the "justice of God"—it means the same thing.[5]

---

[4] G. E. Ladd, "A Theology of the New Testament," p. 439.

[5] I am indebted to Christopher Marshall for these insights. "Beyond Retribution," pp.35ff. See also Robert Brinsmead:
http://www.bobbrinsmead.com/t_The_SCANDAL_OF_GODS_JUSTICE-Pt1.html

The English language has the word group "righteous, righteousness and right-wise," and another word group "just, justification and justify." The first group is derived from the Anglo-Saxon, while the second is from the Latin. The word righteousness is generally reserved for church and "God-talk." Justice is used to discuss concrete social and political issues on earth.

These differences tend to confuse the fact that the Bible does not use one word for righteousness and another for justice. The Old Testament has one word, *sadaq*, for righteousness and justice. New Testament Greek also has one word *dikaiosune*. Thus, "justice is righteousness and righteousness is justice."

Christopher Marshall:

> "[I]n contemporary English language, 'righteousness' and 'justice' have quite distinct connotations. 'Righteousness' carries the sense of personal ethical purity and religious piety (indeed, the term 'righteousness' is virtually obsolete in secular discourse), while 'justice' relates to public judicial fairness and equality of rights. One belongs to the private, moral, religious realm, the other to the public, political, legal realm. But this is not necessarily so in the Bible."[6]

This means that when we read about the righteousness of God in the Bible, we are reading about His justice! We are not reading about God's inner purity. We are reading about a practiced justice. It's about where God is "getting His hands dirty."

---

[6] Marshall, "Beyond Retribution," p. 36

Two Kinds of Justice

Paul tells us that there are two kinds of justice–righteousness; the justice of God and the justice of the law.

> [30] What shall we say then? That Gentiles, who did not pursue righteousness, have attained to righteousness, even *the righteousness of faith*; [31] but Israel, pursuing *the law of righteousness*, has not attained to the law of righteousness. (Romans 9:30–31 NKJV)

Earlier in this book, Paul took great pains to distinguish between these two kinds of righteousness–justice.

> [19] Now we know that whatever the law says, it says to those who are under the law, that every mouth may be stopped, and all the world may become guilty before God. [20] Therefore by the deeds of the law no flesh will be justified in His sight, for by the law *is* the knowledge of sin. [21] But now *the righteousness of God apart from the law is revealed*, being witnessed by the Law and the Prophets, [22] even *the righteousness of God*, through faith in Jesus Christ, to all and on all who believe. (Romans 3:19–22 NKJV)

So there we have a clear contrast and distinction between the righteousness–justice of the law and the justice–righteousness of God. In fact, in Romans 1:15–17 Paul defines the Gospel that saves as "the righteousness of God."

So we need to understand this: "The righteousness of God [is] apart from the law"!

So what's the difference between the two? Before we move forward, remember that we are determining what "justice" means. If it's about restoring people to proper working order, setting things right, then this means that when God manifests His justice through His judgments, only restoration can result! Universal restoration is the only result. This leaves no room to interpret hell as being never-ending damnation! If hell is what happens to the people of the nations during the final judgement of God to bring about His justice, then it must be about a restoration of the "lost"—setting them into proper working order.

Let's look more at the difference between the two kinds of righteous-justice; that of law and that of God.

There are two kinds of justice or two ways in which doing the right thing is understood. These run right through the Old Testament literature and stand in a real tension to each other.

The first, legal kind of justice, the justice–righteousness of the Law, is all about rewards and punishments, an eye for an eye, or pay-back justice. In Deuteronomy 28, we see Moses saying that those who obey all the commandments get blessed and those who don't obey them carefully get cursed. But as Paul tells his readers in his letter to the Galatians, the justice–righteousness of the law was a temporary, educational regime which was imposed on minors until they became of age. (See Chapter 3:21–25). We are no longer under this law (Romans 6:14; 10:4).

The Old Testament, however, also portrays another kind of justice. It is featured in stories of God's mighty acts on behalf of His people. It is often sung about in the Psalms. But above all, it is a justice which is championed by the Old Testament prophets. This is a justice is about doing the right thing in terms of being faithful to a relationship—which the Old Testament often calls a covenant. It is this justice that Paul refers to when he discusses the Gospel and states "the righteousness of God apart from the law is revealed, being *witnessed by the Law and the Prophets*" (Romans 3:22).

So what's so different about this second kind of justice–righteousness?

Professor G. E. Ladd informs us that righteousness involves "a relationship rather than an ethical quality... Basically, 'righteousness' is a concept of *relationship*... It is not a word designating personal ethical character, but faithfulness to a relationship."[7]

We would now enter into the Catholic–Protestant debate here. Catholicism insists that to be righteous or just means to be "made righteous" in behaviour. Protestants say no! For us to be righteous, or just, as far as God is concerned is to be "declared" righteous, in that all the righteous behaviour and works of Jesus are transferred to the believer by faith and in this way, we are considered righteous.

This debate between being "made" or "declared" righteous is misplaced. How? Both assume that righteousness or justice is an ethical–behavioural concept (synonymous with goodness). So then Catholicism and Protestantism are simply arguing about whether God legally declares sinners good on the basis of the works of Jesus or whether He actually makes them good!

However, if the term justice–righteousness is not an ethical–behavioural term and is instead a relational one, then to declare or make righteous misses the point!

In the Bible, justice–righteousness centres on restoring relationships. It's about covenant faithfulness on the part of God to keep and restore His promises.

---

[7] G. E. Ladd, "A Theology of the New Testament," pp. 439–440

Nehemiah speaks of God's covenant faithfulness:

> [7] "You are the LORD God, who chose Abram… and you made a covenant with him to give… [8] You have kept your promise because you are righteous [just, *sadaq*]. (Nehemiah 9:7–8)

Here we can see that justice–righteousness is directly connected to covenant faithfulness. God entered into covenant relationship with Abraham and made promises to him. When God was faithful to His covenant promises, He was found to be just–righteous!

So we can see that justice–righteousness is about faithfulness in keeping promises.

When we read that the Gospel is about the righteousness of God, we are really seeing His faithfulness to keep His promises. God entered into relationship with Abraham and He demonstrates His justice–righteousness when He keeps the promises He made to him!

Justice–righteousness focuses on relationship. God is shown to keep His covenant and maintain relationships and this in the face of very bad human behaviour!

> [33] In all that has happened to us, you have remained righteous [just, *sadaq*]; you have acted ***faithfully***, while we acted wickedly. (Nehemiah 9:33)

God's justice–righteousness is in spite of bad behaviour! God's righteousness is focused on relationship. He makes covenant promises and because of this relationship, He keeps His word regardless of our behaviour.

Justice in the Bible is about God, the judge, intervening to rescue, save and deliver.

We see this dynamic when Jesus tells a story about an unjust judge (Luke 18:1–8). This story tells us something about the role of a judge in Bible days. A woman kept coming to this particular unjust judge to seek justice. As an unjust judge, he kept sending her away until:

> ⁵ Yet because this widow keeps bothering me, I will see that she gets justice. (Luke 18:5)

We see here that judges were expected to take direct action personally; not just make decisions! They were expected to get their hands dirty and act on behalf of the oppressed. They didn't just sit at a bench and make decisions and declarations.

Judges in Bible days took action to set the oppressed free.

As we have seen, God's righteousness in the Old Testament was rooted in covenant faithfulness. Because of this, Israel could count on God rescuing them whenever they were in self-induced trouble.

God's covenant faithfulness [His justice–righteousness!] resulted in many rescues!

God's judgments were manifestations of His justice. We read that God judges on the basis of righteousness (Ps 96:13; 98:9). And passages like these in Isaiah 11 and Psalm 72 show God's role as judge involving acting faithfully for the needy and the oppressed:

> ⁴ But with *righteousness He* will *judge the needy,*
> *with justice He* will give decisions *for the poor* of the earth.
> (Isaiah 11:4)

> ¹ Endow the king with *your justice* O God,
> the royal son with *your righteousness.*
> ² May He *judge* your people *in righteousness,*
> your *afflicted ones with justice.* (Psalm 72:1–2)

The words "judge," "justice" and "righteousness" are placed in direct parallel; they mean the same thing. From these verses we can see that the role of a judge was to show justice which means the same thing as to show righteousness. These words are the same. God's justice–righteousness targets those afflicted.

> [16] But the LORD Almighty will be exalted by *His justice*, and the holy God will show Himself *holy* by *is righteousness*. (Isaiah 5:16 NIV *1984*)

> [16] But the LORD Almighty will be exalted by *His justice*, and the *holy* God will be proved holy by His *righteous acts*.(Isaiah 5:16 NIV *2011*)

As we compare this verse in both versions of the NIV we can see that the word "righteousness" is later translated as "righteous acts." Did you notice that the words justice and righteousness or righteous acts are a demonstration not only of the righteousness of God but also of His holiness? It is very hard to separate all these ideas in the Bible. But what we have seen is that all these words have been given a retributive flavour in the Western church—but they don't imply this at all in the Bible. For now, we can see that the righteousness of God in the Old Testament is about His "righteous acts."

Isaiah 51 is revealing:

> [5] My *righteousness* draws near speedily,
> my *salvation* is on the way,
> and my arm will bring *justice* to the nations.
> The islands will look to me
> and wait in hope for my arm. (Isaiah 51:5)

And

Psalm 71:

> [2] In **your righteousness, rescue** me and **deliver** me;
> turn your ear to me and **save** me. (Psalm 71:2)

Just, righteous, holiness, judge, salvation, rescue, deliver and save—they are all connected; they all describe what the justice–righteousness of God is about.

Isaiah summarises it for us nicely:

> [18] Yet the LORD longs to be *gracious* to you;
> therefore He will rise up to show you *compassion.*
> For the LORD is a *God of justice.* (Isaiah 30:18)

It is clear: God's justice is not damnatory, instead it releases grace and compassion.

If this is clearly the case, this means that when God's justice demands that He acts against evil through His judgements, that restoration is the only thing that He has in mind. Remember that the Hebrew word for "just" means to fix that which is broken; to restore; it's never "just" to torture or totally destroy.

We have an interesting but significant use of the Hebrew word, *sadaq,* in Daniel 8:14. God's sanctuary had been trodden down and defiled by the evil little horn power. It was no longer in proper working order! God promised:

> [14] And he answered him, "For two thousand three hundred evenings and mornings; then the sanctuary shall be *restored to its rightful state*." (Daniel 8:14 NRSV)

The underlined phrase is all one word in the original language. It comes from the niphal form of the verb *sadaq.* The word *sadaq* means to be in proper working order. God's sanctuary was no longer in proper working order and God promised to "justify" it—that is "restore to its rightful state." So there we have it. When God releases His righteousness–justice, that which is broken gets restored to its rightful state!

Paul brings this all together in Romans 3 where he states that the righteousness–justice of God was supremely manifested on the Cross when God took the Sin–tyrant to task to set the world free from its control and oppression.

When we compare Romans 3:3 and 3:5, it appears that God's faithfulness and righteousness mean the same thing. This fits perfectly with the Old Testament picture. At its root, righteousness–justice is a relational concept. Paul tells us that sin is a universal problem—"all have sinned"—and so the solution is that God takes the initiative to set things right; the result is all things are to be justified—that is restored back to proper working order! "All have sinned"—all are "broken"—and all require fixing or restoring. So God, through His righteousness–justice manifested by Jesus on the Cross, takes action to step in and rescue, save, deliver and restore the human race. This is the crux of Paul's argument in Romans 3:19–26.

Consider the flow of Paul's thought:

> [23] Since ***all have sinned*** and fall short of the glory of God; [24] ***they are now justified*** [that is restored back to proper working order] by His grace as a gift, through the redemption that is in Christ Jesus (Romans 3:23–24 NRSV)

Consider how the New International Version renders these verses:

> [23] For ***all have sinned*** and fall short of the glory of God, [24]***and all are justified*** freely by His grace through the redemption that came by Christ Jesus. (Romans 3:23–24)

The same all that have sinned and are broken are now in the process of being restored back to working order, and the death of Jesus was pivotal to all of this!

Read it again carefully. Universal salvation is the logical conclusion insofar as the death of Jesus is concerned!

Through death, Jesus absorbs sin into himself to eliminate it and set us free. In Christ, God acts as the faithful judge in covenant loyalty to vindicate the oppressed: the world held captive by sin. The power of sin has been broken over humanity; we need not obey it any longer (Romans 6).

But there's more involved in restoring things to proper working order.

It is not just humans as individuals that are restored—justified. Human relationships are also restored. The righteousness of God has a social dimension to it as well[8].

First the Old Testament.

> [9] "This is what the LORD Almighty said: '***Administer true justice; show mercy and compassion*** to one another.
> [10] ***Do not oppress*** the widow or the fatherless, the foreigner or the poor. Do not plot evil against each other.'
> (Zechariah 7:9–10)

God administers true justice to people and then calls for those people to do likewise for their fellow man. Justice begets justice.

---

[8] For a succinct but perceptive examination of justice in the Old Testament see Sharon L. Baker, article "The Repetition of Reconciliation: Satisfying Justice, Mercy, and Forgiveness" in Stricken by God, 220–240.

Sharon L Baker:

> "We see then that mercy describes the nature of justice. As such, it includes maintaining the cause of the needy (Ps. 140:12; Ezekiel 34:16), giving food to the hungry (Ps. 146:7), rescuing the oppressed (Isa. 1:17; Jer. 22:3) and peacemaking (Isaiah 42:1–4; Jer. 22:3). In these verses and others, mercy and justice complement each other so that in doing mercy, we also do justice. In other words, justice stimulates mercy, and mercy serves and establishes justice."[9]

When God establishes righteousness through Jesus, it is not only about personal restoration; it is to create a restored community. This is why Paul continues his discussion on righteousness and includes restored human relationships in Romans 3:29—which he takes up again in detail in Romans 12–16, applying the justice of God demonstrated on the Cross in community relationships!

God's righteousness is a community–forming righteousness where social justice results. This is central to the message of the prophets in the Old Testament.

Jesus focuses on this aspect of justice–righteousness in detail.[10] Remember my main point: since God's justice is only restorative, restoration is the only end result when He judges sin. People are not completely destroyed or tortured endlessly.

---

[9] Sharon L Baker, Razing Hell, p. 86.

[10] I am indebted to Dr. Darren W. Snyder Belousek for what follows: "Atonement, Justice and Peace," pp 31ff.

Jesus on Justice

Jesus said that he did not come to destroy the law but to fulfil it in terms of righteousness–justice. See Matthew 5:17–20. In so doing, Jesus rejected the trajectory of retribution and retaliation inherent in the law. He cites retributive elements within the law and clearly repudiates them.

Moses in the law said "an eye for an eye"—clear retribution; but Jesus wiped that all away. Matthew 5:38–42. The examples Jesus gives— turning the other cheek, giving the cloak and going the extra mile— all illustrate the point of not returning "like for like" to those who treat us unjustly. Instead of the law of retribution, treatment back in kind, Jesus calls us to the righteousness–justice of the Kingdom which is: "do unto others as you would have them do unto you"(Luke 6:31).

Jesus speaks out against the retributive justice of the law when he calls people to show kindness to enemies even though the Old Testament writings clearly call for Israel to kill such enemies in certain circumstances. See Deuteronomy 20. Jesus calls us to love others who don't love us, to lend to those who take from us, bless those who seek to harm us. Clearly Jesus repudiated the retributive elements of justice within the law and instead calls us to "seek the righteousness–justice of God" which we have just outlined.

I will end this discussion on God's justice with one more passage.

Jesus had just healed a large crowd. Matthew tells us that this healing illustrated a principle of God:

> [17] *This was to fulfill* what was spoken through
> *the prophet* Isaiah:
> [18] "Here is my servant whom I have chosen,
> the one I love, in whom I delight;
> I will put my Spirit on him,

and *he will proclaim justice to the nations*.
¹⁹ He will not quarrel or cry out;
no one will hear his voice in the streets.
²⁰ A bruised reed he will not break,
and a smoldering wick he will not snuff out,
till he has brought justice through to victory.
²¹ In his name the nations will put their hope."
(Matthew 12:17–21)

Jesus came to fulfil the law and the prophets. In this case, Matthew is furnishing us with an example of how Jesus fulfilled the prophets by telling us exactly how God's justice works. Jesus healed the crowds and he did this to show us what God's justice is all about.

God's justice results in healing! There is no malice with Jesus (who perfectly displays our Father). He will not quarrel about it. He has no need to break those who are "broken" even more, but has a plan to heal all! He will continue to heal UNTIL He has brought justice through to ultimate victory for the nations! This is powerful and needs to be read with the full force Matthew intends.

Justice results in victory and healing for the nations, and Jesus will continue on this mission until all nations have put their hope in him.

Justice can only manifest in healing and restoration. When Jesus meets a sin-stricken, sick person, he manifests God's justice when he is healing that person.

Here we find a major reason I am convinced about universal restoration.

The justice of God demands that He deal with evil. But the result is healing; not breaking people further or snuffing them out!

God's justice is not about damnation or retribution. It's about restoration because the nature of God's justice is to fix that which was broken!

CHAPTER FOUR

The Streaming Nations: Destination Eden Restored

I was first introduced to the idea of Universalism back in 1984 during my last year in study at College before entering into full time pastoral ministry. Dr Turner presented a lecture on the Old Testament that has stayed with me. He opened this lecture by saying, "Today we are going to look at universalism in the prophets." This immediately grabbed my attention. He went on to point out how the later prophets emphasised the idea that Israelite nationalism was giving way to Universalism. Once he shared all the related passages from those prophets, I was dumbfounded.

Five years later, I went back to Seminary and started my post-graduate study. I majored in what is called Biblical Apocalyptic and Eschatology. These are just big words that describe the doctrine of end time events with great focus on symbolic books like Daniel and Revelation. Whilst working towards this degree, I was asked to write a thesis on the Two Witnesses of Revelation 11.

As I prepared this paper, I was becoming more convinced that universal salvation could actually be possible. That was back in 1988! As I immersed myself into my studies, I came to the conclusion that Revelation described an end-time, world-wide conversion to Jesus.

But it was not until 2011 that I finally accepted that universal restoration was a major theme of the Bible. A monumental book by Dr. Robin Parry, "The Evangelical Universalist" brought me over the line. In this one book, Parry combined what I had learned about universalism in the prophets and what John wrote in Revelation. Bingo! I was finally convinced, but it nearly took 30 years!

Much of what follows combines what I learned from my personal studies with what Dr. Parry wrote in his book.

In this chapter we will trace the way God leads all nations to himself into the New Jerusalem. As we consider this we will notice that there is an interaction between theodicy and universalism. That is, God deals with evil not by destroying the nations but by cleansing all nations from evil within.

As we travel through the Bible we nearly find a love-hate relationship between God and the nations.

On the one hand, Isaiah can say the following about the nations:

> [1]Come near, you *nations*, and listen;
> pay attention, you *peoples*!
> Let *the earth* hear, and all that is in it,
> *the world*, and all that comes out of it!
> [2]The **LORD** *is angry with all nations*;
> His wrath is on all their armies.
> He will totally destroy them, (Isaiah 34:1–2)

The words "nations, peoples, earth, world" are all different ways of speaking about universal activity. God's justice demands that He responds to universal evil with universal wrath and judgment, and it really seems from these verses that it is curtains for all nations.

And yet other passages in the same book lead us in a different direction.

> [22] *Turn to me and be saved,*
> *all* the *ends* of the *earth*!
> For I am God, and there is no other.
> [23] By myself I have sworn,
> from my mouth has gone forth in righteousness
> a word that shall not return:
> "*To me every knee* shall bow,
> every tongue *shall swear*."
>
> [24] *Only in the LORD*, it shall be said of me,
> are *righteousness* and strength;
> *all who were incensed against him*
> *shall come* to him and be ashamed.
> (Isaiah 45:22–24 NRSV)

On the one hand, we have God's universal war on evil, and on the other hand, we have proclamations that all nations who were once at war with God eventually bend the knee and turn to God in salvation, swearing that righteousness is in Yahweh alone. All the ends of the earth turn to God ashamed at their warring with the One who saves.

God declares war on evil. But He does so through inner cleansing that results in restoration!

Salvation of the Nations

The phrase "all the nations" is a significant one in the Bible. The "nations" are first mentioned and identified as the clans and families of Noah's three boys.

> [32] These are the clans of Noah's sons, according to their lines of descent, within their nations. From these *the nations spread out over the earth after the flood.* (Genesis 10:32)

Earlier, we learned that their multiplying and filling the earth was part of God's original plan. Compare Genesis 1:28 and 10:32.

We also saw that the nations came against the universal plan of God to fill the earth.

> [4] Then they said, "Come, let us build ourselves a city, with a tower that reaches to the heavens, so that we may make a name for ourselves; *otherwise we will be scattered over the face of the whole earth.*" (Genesis 11:4)

At this point, God intervenes with a judgment. He confuses their language and sets them back on the path of the Edenic universal blessing.

> [8] So the LORD scattered them from there over all the earth (Genesis 11:8)

Judgment is about God bringing the world back on track to receive His universal blessing. While man often perceives what God is doing as bad, God intends it for good. So a pattern has been set: Judgment is unto salvation.

But the story begins to change somewhat. At first we see God dealing with the nations corporately—with humanity as a whole. But now the plot begins to change. We are introduced to Abraham. God will now deal with the nations through an individual. And so the story of universal salvation takes centre stage.

> ³ I will bless those who bless you,
> and whoever curses you I will curse;
> and *all peoples on Earth*
> *will be blessed through you.*" (Genesis 12:3)

"All peoples" will be blessed through Abraham. All means all! God did not tell Abraham that all people of the earth may, could or might be blessed! God told him that all people *will* be blessed through him as an individual.

God begins the process of bringing the world back to Eden through one man, Abraham.

How would the blessing of all nations actually come to pass?

How will all nations be blessed through Abraham? This is what the rest of the Bible is about.

We will see that this process involves a war on inherent evil that cleanses and restores all humanity.

This "blessing" comes into being through Abraham's seed.

> ⁴ I will make your descendants as numerous as the stars in the sky and will give them all these lands, and *through your seed all nations* on earth will be blessed (Genesis 26:4)

This same promise is deliberately emphasised throughout the Bible: Genesis 18:18; 22:18; 26:4; 28:14; Psalm 72:17; Isaiah 19:24–25; Jeremiah 4:2; Zechariah 8:13; Galatians 3:16, 8.

How was the blessing of all nations going to manifest through the seed of Abraham?

The Nations Will Stream into the Temple of God

The Old Testament indicates that the nations would enter into a relationship with the God of Israel after seeing how He delivers Israel time and again. When God delivers Israel, the nations come to see that His name is great.[11] When God acts to rescue these who are called His people, the result is that "all the earth will see the salvation of our God" (Isaiah 52:10 cf. 40:3–5).

> [1]This is what Isaiah son of Amoz saw concerning Judah and Jerusalem:
> [2] *In the last days* the mountain of *the LORD's temple* will be established as the highest of the mountains; it will be exalted above the hills, and *all nations will stream to it.*
>
> [5] Come, descendants of Jacob,
> *let us walk in the light of the LORD.* (Isaiah 2:2,5)

Why does Isaiah call Israel, the seed, to walk in the light of the Lord? What bearing does this have on the nations streaming to God?

> [1]Arise, shine, for *your light has come*,
> ad the glory of the LORD rises upon you.
> [2] See, darkness covers the earth
> and thick darkness is over the peoples,
> but the LORD rises upon you
> and His glory appears over you.
> [3] *Nations will come to your light* (Isaiah 60:1–3)

---

[11] Exodus 9:16; 2 Samuel 7:23; Nehemiah 9:10; Psalm 106:8; Isaiah 63:10, 12; Jeremiah 32:20; Daniel 9:15.

Isaiah calls Israel to walk in the light of the Lord because the nations will be drawn by it and stream into God's house, the Temple, as a result.

Jeremiah is direct:

> [1] "If you, Israel, will return,
> then return to me,"
> declares the LORD.
> "If you put your detestable idols out of my sight
> and no longer go astray,
> [2] and if in a truthful, just and righteous way
> you swear, 'As surely as the LORD lives,'
> ***then the nations will invoke blessings by him***
> and in him they will boast." Jeremiah 4:1–2

Jeremiah contains a clear reference to the divine promise given to Abraham: all the nations will be blessed! If Israel the seed remains faithful to God, then the nations would see their light and be drawn to God as a result and experience the universal blessing given to Adam, to Noah's sons and then to Abraham!

The idea of the nations flowing to the God of Israel to worship at the Temple is picked up repeatedly in the prophets; especially in Isaiah.

The nations will be drawn to the God of Israel, to His Temple, and bring Him gifts in worship:

> [7] At that time gifts will be brought to the LORD Almighty
> from a people tall and smooth-skinned,
> from a people feared far and wide,
> an aggressive nation of strange speech,
> whose land is divided by rivers—the gifts will be brought to
> Mount Zion, the place of the Name of the LORD Almighty.
> (Isaiah 18:7)

And:

> [18] "...[I] am about to come and gather the people of all
> nations and languages, and they will come and see my glory.
>
> [21] And I will select some of them also to be priests and
> Levites," says the LORD.
> [22] "As the new heavens and the new earth that I make will
> endure before me," declares the LORD, "so will your name
> and descendants endure. [23] From one New Moon to another
> and from one Sabbath to another, ***all mankind will come and
> bow down before me,*** " says the LORD.
> (Isaiah 66:18, 21–23)

God promises to gather all nations. Some would even become priests
and Levites! By the time we reach the "new heavens and the new
earth," all mankind will come and bow down and worship the God of
Israel.

This is how God planned to bless all nations through Israel. The
nations would see Israel walking in the light of God and be drawn to
the light as a result. But the national seed of Abraham failed in this
calling. They did not always walk in God's light. It seems like God's
plan for the nations has failed. But it is then the prophets begin to
speak of a Seed who will successfully heed this calling and fulfil it.

Here's a hint of how it will happen.

> [10] In that day the Root of Jesse will stand as a banner for the
> peoples; the nations will rally to him, and his resting place
> will be glorious.
> [12] He will raise a banner for the nations
> and gather the exiles of Israel;

he will assemble the scattered people of Judah
from the four quarters of the earth. (Isaiah 11:10–12)

I can't help myself—just look at this most marvellous promise! The "Root of Jesse" is Jesus!

Paul quotes this verse and applies it directly to Jesus:

> [12] And again, Isaiah says,
> "The Root of Jesse will spring up,
> one who will arise to rule over the nations;
> in him the Gentiles will hope." (Romans 15:12)

Isaiah and Paul say that "the nations" will rally to Jesus, to his resting place! Jesus will be a banner for all nations together with Israel and Judah! What is this banner that the nations see that draws them?

We will have to jump forward here.

> [32] And I, when I am lifted up from the earth, will draw all people to myself." [33] He said this to show the kind of death he was going to die. (John 12:32–33)

The Cross is the banner of Jesus; it *will* draw all people to Jesus! He did not say that he could, but rather that he will.

We will discuss this more later. For now, we are still laying down the foundation.

It is not only Isaiah that speaks about a universal gathering of all nations for the purpose of salvation. Consider what the Psalms say about the destiny of the nations.

Universal Salvation in the Psalms

Many Psalms call the nations to worship the God of Israel and speak about a time when this will happen.

Look at Psalm 117. Look at its entire message:

> ¹ Praise the LORD, all you nations;
> extol him, all you peoples.
> ² For great is His love toward us,
> and the faithfulness of the LORD endures forever.
> Praise the LORD. (Psalm 117)

It is clear. The Psalmist calls the whole world to worship God, saying that His love and faithfulness extends to all; not just Israel!

Again:

We have another entire Psalm dedicated to this same idea.

> ¹ May God be **gracious** to us [Israel] and **bless us** [Israel]
> and make His face shine on us—
> ² so that your ways may be known on earth,
> your **salvation** among **all nations**. (Psalm 67:1–2)

Now this is important. The writer equates God's grace and blessing upon Israel with their salvation! He tells us that when the world sees God's grace, blessing and salvation upon Israel, the world is seeing the ways of God. And the result?

> ³ **May the peoples praise you**, God;
> may all the peoples praise you.
> ⁴ May the nations be glad and sing for joy,
> for you rule the peoples with equity
> and guide the nations of the earth.

⁵ May the peoples praise you, God;
may *all the peoples praise you*.
⁶ The land yields its harvest;
God, our *God, blesses us*.
⁷ May God bless us still,
*so that all the ends of the earth will fear [in context =
praise] him*. (Psalm 67:3)

Did you notice that the blessing of Abraham on Israel has the purpose of drawing all nations into the same blessing? "I will bless you and in your seed all the nations of the earth shall be blessed!"

Please don't forget that God is not calling a representation of peoples from all the nations; the text specifically defines all nations as "all the peoples"! Not some of all peoples; not most people! All!

There is a call and an intention. The text says "may" they come and praise God.

Then "may" becomes "will"!

So this is the call. Is it fulfilled? Do all nations eventually heed the call? Do all the nations come to God and worship him?

> ⁹ *All the nations you have made*
> *WILL come and worship before you, Lord*;
> they *WILL* bring glory to your name.
> ¹⁰ For you are great and do marvelous deeds;
> you alone are God. (Psalm 86:9–10)

Can it be?! Yes it is! The call is heeded. Hallelujah!

The Psalms are clear: the blessing of Abraham will be fulfilled. All nations will turn to the Lord and worship Him!

So as the nations see the blessing of God [grace and salvation] upon Israel, they end up coming to God and praising Him. It is in this way that the blessing of Abraham becomes the blessing of all nations!

The call is heeded. All nations will come and worship the God of Israel because of some marvellous deeds He does. What are these marvellous deeds?

> [4] *All the kings of the earth shall praise You, O LORD,*
> When they hear the words of Your mouth.
> [5] Yes, they shall sing of *the ways of the LORD,*
> For great *is* the glory of the LORD. (Psalm 138:4–5 NKJV)

When they hear God's words and see His mighty ways and deeds, then ALL the kings of the earth will—not may or might—praise the God of Israel!

And there are so many more passages:

> [7] For God is the King of all the earth;
> sing to Him a psalm of praise.
>
> [8] God reigns over the nations;
> God is seated on His holy throne.
> [9] The *nobles of the nations assemble*
> *as the people of the God of Abraham,*
> *for* *the kings of the earth belong to God*;
> He is greatly exalted. (Psalm 47:7–9)

The nobles of the nations will be as the people of the God of Abraham! Please let that sink in.

It's all over the Psalms:

> ¹⁰ May the kings of Tarshish and of distant shores
> bring tribute to him.
> May the kings of Sheba and Seba
> present him gifts.
> ¹¹ May all kings bow down to him
> and ***all nations serve him***. (Psalm 72:10–11)

And again:

> ²¹ So the name of the LORD will be declared in Zion
> and His praise in Jerusalem
> ²² when **the peoples and the kingdoms
> assemble to worship the LORD**. (Psalm 102:21–22)

And here is one of the most radical passages in Bible:

> ²⁷ ***All the ends of the world***
> **Shall** remember and **turn to the LORD,**
> And **all** the families of the nations
> **Shall worship** before You.
> ²⁸ For the kingdom *is* the LORD's,
> And He rules over the nations.
>
> ²⁹ **All those who go down to the dust**
> Shall bow before Him,
> Even he who cannot keep himself alive.
> (Psalm 22:27–29 NKJV)

The Psalmist is talking about "all the ends of the world," "all the families of the nations"—ALL! How much more universalistic can it be? Not most of the world or many families—but all!

"All" shall what? "All" will (not may!) turn to the Lord! They will all come to faith in the God of Israel.

And the best news is that "all" includes all those who die—they bow too! Here even the dead come to faith and turn to God.

This is scandalous grace!

Israel was to be the light unto the nation, but Israel fails to fulfil the calling. Isaiah takes this up in detail. The plan unfolds—more of it is revealed.

The Two Servants of God

Israel's light–bearing, servant–mission to the nations is described in detail in Isaiah. This mission is found in what is called "the four Servant Songs" (Isaiah 42:1–7; 49:1–9; 50:4–11; 52:13–53:12).

So what's so important about these servant songs, and how do they relate to universal restoration of all nations? There is a clear story contained in these four servant songs. I will unfold the story found in Isaiah 41–53 as simply as I can. Here we go.

The four Servant Songs speak about God's call on Israel's life. As a servant, Israel was called to bring the nations to the God of Israel. But these songs make it clear that the servant Israel failed in this calling. Then there is a shift in the servant's identity. The servant Israel, as a nation, is replaced by an individual servant who becomes the Suffering Servant of Isaiah 53. It is in this individual–servant that the promise of Abraham comes to fulfilment. Isaiah lays the foundation of universal restoration in Jesus as the Seed of Abraham and the Servant of God. And it is this idea which is taken up in the New Testament!

Let's unpack this in detail.

The first Servant Song is found in Chapter 42 of Isaiah. But the identity of this servant is clearly laid out in Chapter 41!

> [8] "But you, *Israel, my servant,*
> Jacob, whom I have chosen,
> you *descendants of Abraham* my friend, (Isaiah 41:8)

Notice here that the servant refers to "descendants"—plural. Clearly, the nation of Israel is the first servant.

This particular servant becomes blind and dumb!

> [19] Who is **blind but my servant,**
> and **deaf like the messenger I send**?
> Who is blind like the one in covenant with me,
> *blind* **like the servant of the LORD**? (Isaiah 42:19)

God has a servant who becomes blind and dumb! This servant is not Jesus!

So what is the mission of servant–national–Israel?

> [1] "Here is my servant, whom I uphold,
> my chosen one in whom I delight;
> I will put my Spirit on him,
> and *he will bring justice to the nations*.
>
> [4] he will not falter or be discouraged
> *till he establishes justice on earth*.
> In his teaching the islands will put their hope."
>
> [6] "*I, the LORD, have called you* in righteousness;
> I will take hold of your hand.
> I will keep you and *will make you*
> *to be a covenant for the people*

> *and a light for the Gentiles,*
> [7] to open eyes that are blind,
> to free captives from prison
> and to release from the dungeon those who sit in darkness.
> (Isaiah 42:1, 4, 6–7)

The first servant has its mission outlined clearly. The role of the first servant is to become a *covenant* for the nations—it seems that Israel functions as mediators of some sort of covenant between the God of Israel and the nations! Servant–Israel becomes a light for the Gentiles. Israel was to bring "justice" on the earth. This justice is clearly described in terms of restoring sight! We have already learned that true justice involves restoration back to proper working order.

The mission of the servant was restoration of all the nations! The nations are blind and so the servant is called to restore sight. The nations are in a prison of darkness and the servant is called to set them free! But notice what happens next.

In verse 19 of this chapter, the servant becomes blind and dumb! Servant–Israel, who was to be a light to the Gentiles and restore their sight, has now become blind (Isaiah 42:16, 18–25). Israel is now in the same position as the nations! Israel now needs servant ministry too. In this state of blindness, they cannot fulfil that calling: they cannot be a source of light to the nations as God called them to be.

She is in foreign captivity as a result of her rebellion and self-induced blindness. Isaiah was written to Israel while she was held in captivity (Isaiah 1:2–4 cf. 42:22–24). Israel is in need of restoration. God promises to restore her. She is in captivity under Babylon as she was in Egypt. So God promises an exodus out of Babylon as well! (Isaiah 43:14–21; 46:8–13)

Please keep in mind that Isaiah 41–53:12 is one complete unit—one unfolding story. The servant Israel has failed its mission. Instead of being a light to the Gentiles and drawing them to God, she has turned to the gods of the nations and finds herself in captivity. Isaiah writes to an Israel in captivity in Babylon, promising rescue (Isaiah 43:41–21). Now Israel has to be fully restored!

But how exactly will Israel be restored? **Isaiah will point out a very important dynamic: Israel's restoration becomes the trigger for all nations to come streaming to God.**

> ¹⁷ But *Israel will be saved by the LORD*
> *with an everlasting salvation;*
> you will never be put to shame or disgraced,
> to ages everlasting. (Isaiah 45:17)

Israel will not remain in captivity. She will be restored–saved!

After Israel is set free and restored:

> ²² *"Turn to me and be saved,*
> *all you ends of the earth;*
> for I am God, and there is no other.
> ²³ By myself I have sworn,
> my mouth has uttered in all integrity
> a word that will not be revoked:
> *Before me every knee will bow;*
> by me every tongue will swear.
> ²⁴ *They will say of me, 'In the LORD alone*
> *are deliverance and strength.'"*
> All who have raged against him
> will come to him and be put to shame.

[25] But all the descendants of Israel
will find deliverance in the LORD
and will make their boast in him. (Isaiah 45:22–25)

I hope you understand the importance of this passage. We looked at it earlier without looking at the context, but now you can see what this is saying within the unfolding logic and narrative of the four Servant Songs! Isaiah is telling us that servant–Israel was failing to be a light to the Gentiles and had turned to other gods, resulting in captivity! But God promised to deliver servant–Israel despite her transgressions, and the result of this salvation is that the nations would turn to the mighty saving hand of the God of Israel! After the world witnesses this mighty salvation, the God of Israel calls out to all the ends of the earth to turn and be saved. And we see clearly that when God calls this time, all turn to the Lord; God vows that every knee will call on Him and be saved—and they all do! All the nations that raged against God declare His righteousness! Wow!

The passage ends in verses 23–25 by connecting the restoration of Israel with the salvation of all the earth. We will examine this again soon.

So How is Servant–Israel Restored?

This is crucial to know since the blessing of the nations is dependent on it!

Servant–national–Israel is replaced by an individual who will become a servant, first to Israel and then to the nations!

God promises to rescue servant–Israel by sending a servant–rescuer from the East.

[8] "Remember this, keep it in mind,
take it to heart, you rebels.
[9] Remember the former things, those of long ago;
I am God, and there is no other; I am God, and there is none like me.
[10] *I make known the end from the beginning [I AM IN CONTROL],* from ancient times, what is still to come.
I say, '*My purpose will stand,* and I will do all that I please.'
[GOD WILL STILL SEND THE SERVANT TO THE NATIONS!]
[11] *From the east* I summon a bird of prey; from a far-off land, *a man to fulfill my purpose.*
What I have said, that I *will bring about; what I have planned,* that I will do.
[12] Listen to me, you stubborn-hearted,
you who are now far from my righteousness.
[13] I am bringing my righteousness near,
it is not far away;
and my salvation will not be delayed.
*I will grant salvation to Zion,
my splendor to Israel.* (Isaiah 46:8–13)

Israel will be saved by "a *man* to fulfil my purpose"

Here we see a shift in the servant's identity. National–servant Israel's task will be taken on by a faithful individual servant who becomes the Suffering Servant of Chapter 53!

Note the crucial transition between the two servants:

[3] *He* said to *me*, "You are *my servant,*
Israel, in whom I will display my splendor."
[4] *But I said,* "I have labored in vain;
I have spent my strength for nothing at all.

Yet what is due me is in the LORD's hand,
and my reward is with my God." (Isaiah 49:3–4)

Here we read of a conversation between a "he" and a "me." It is clear that "he" is God. But who is "me"? "Me" is clearly "my servant." This "me"–servant seems to feel that what he is doing is a waste of time.

Who is this servant? Is it Israel? No!

> ⁵ And now *the LORD says*—
> He who *formed me in the womb to be His servant*
> *to bring Jacob back to Him*
> and *gather Israel to Himself,*
> for I am honored in the eyes of the LORD
> and my God has been my strength—
> ⁶ He says:
> "It is too small a thing for *you to be my servant*
> *to restore the tribes of Jacob*
> and bring back those of Israel I have kept.
> I will also *make you a light for the Gentiles,*
> that *My salvation may reach to the ends of the earth."*
> (Isaiah 49:5–6)

Bingo! Can you see this? This servant will restore the first servant Israel who is currently in captivity. And in this, the promise to Abraham is fulfilled: "that my salvation may reach the ends of the earth." This individual–servant not only restores Israel–national–servant, but also becomes a light for the Gentiles—so that God's salvation will reach the ends of the earth! The promise made to Abraham will be fulfilled! The mission will carry on!

Israel as a nation is no longer called the servant. The title and responsibilities are transferred and fulfilled by the individual servant—who the New Testament clearly identifies as Jesus!

Through Jesus, all nations will be [not might be!] blessed. This blessing is called the Gospel. Please read Galatians 3:8 and 16 to this point.

So national–Israel is never called the servant again in Isaiah! It's now the individual—the Suffering Servant!

In verses 4–6 we read of an individual servant who rescues Israel–servant. We explicitly read of a transfer of mission and responsibilities onto this individual.

> [8] This is what the LORD says:
> "I will keep you and will ***make you***
> ***to be a covenant for the people,***
> ***to restore*** the land
> and to reassign its desolate inheritances,
> [9] to ***say to the captives, 'Come out,'***
> ***and to those in darkness, 'Be free!'***
>
> [12] See, ***they will come from afar—***
> some from the north, some from the west,
> some from the region of Aswan."
>
> [13] Shout for joy, you heavens;
> rejoice, you earth;
> burst into song, you mountains!
> ***For the LORD comforts His people***
> and will have compassion on His afflicted ones. (Isaiah 49:8–9, 12–13)

The individual servant does for Israel what Israel was to do for the nations.

Servant–Israel was to be a covenant for the nations, and now Servant–Jesus becomes a covenant for Israel.

Servant–Israel was to set the peoples free from prison and darkness, and now Servant–Jesus sets Servant–Israel free from prison and darkness.

And Servant–Jesus is also a light for the Gentiles and salvation for the nations!

Servant–Jesus knows what his rescue mission will involve. We now move into the third Servant Song. The story continues to unfold.

> [4] The Sovereign LORD has given *me* [the new servant in context] a well-instructed tongue, to know the word that sustains the weary. He wakens me morning by morning, wakens my ear to listen like one being instructed.
> [5] The Sovereign LORD has opened my ears;
> ***I have not been rebellious, I have not turned away.***
> [COMPARED TO SERVANT–ISRAEL!]
> [6] ***I offered my back to those who beat me,***
> my cheeks to those who ***pulled out my beard***;
> I did not hide my face from ***mocking and spitting***
> (Isaiah 50:4–8, 10)

Suffering awaits this servant.

But that's not all!

The individual servant comes to Israel's rescue. He is called a servant alongside Israel for the sake of identification with them. Israel is suffering; and so the servant enters the scene (history) and suffers alongside of them. He shares with Israel in their pain and suffering.

Watch this! The Old Testament prophets speak of this particular captivity and release of Israel in terms of "death and resurrection" (See Ezekiel 37; Hosea 6:2; Isaiah 26:19). So the individual comes onto the scene and identifies with them in the process of setting them free. He joins in with them with his own death and resurrection in order to empathise with them and set them free. The servant in Isaiah 53 dies and comes back to life symbolising the eventual release from captivity! And look at what happens. After the death and vindication of the Suffering Servant is over, Israel is restored. Chapter 54 talks of their restoration, and Chapter 55 talks of all the nations streaming to God as a result! Wow! Watch!

The servant suffers, dies and comes back to life in Chapter 53.

Then we read:

> [1] *"Sing*, barren woman,
> you who never bore a child;
> *burst into song*, shout for joy, (Isaiah 54:1)

The barren woman who never bore a child is called to rejoice! She is free as a result of the death and resurrection of the Servant! Remember that chapters and verses are something we have added. There are no chapters and verses in the original text. This verse directly follows on from the Suffering Servant being vindicated, brought back to life and rejoicing over the results of his death!

Israel is called to rejoice. First God tells Israel that they are free. Then He turns to the nations!

> [3] Give ear and come to me;
> listen, that you may live.
> I will make an everlasting covenant with you,
> my faithful love promised to David.
> [4] See, I have made him a witness to the peoples,
> a ruler and commander of the peoples.
> [5] Surely you will summon nations you know not,
> *and nations you do not know*
> *will come running to you,*

> because of the LORD your God,
> the Holy One of Israel,
> *for He has endowed you with splendor.*" Isaiah 55:3–5

Can you see it? As a result of the death and resurrection of the Suffering Servant, Israel is restored, and the nations come streaming in!

I'm not sure why anyone would say that the Bible doesn't speak about universal restoration! I declare that this is one of its central themes! Paul calls the blessing of all as the Gospel in Galatians 3:8.

Let's look at the way Isaiah interweaves judgment into this scenario.

Destiny of the Nations in Isaiah: Judgment unto Salvation

Isaiah blends the salvation of Israel and the nations with judgment unto salvation. Theodicy plays a role here. God shows Himself to be just in the face of evil by declaring war on evil, dealing with it by eradicating it, and leaving human beings restored!

In Isaiah, we find that Israel leaves God and ends up in captivity—judged by God. But this judgment is not their end. An exodus of grace follows the temporal judgment and it is by means of an individual–servant who takes upon himself the nation's identity, role and destiny. This part of Israel's story is about captivity and restoration; death to life! The servant comes, shares in their suffering, and sets them free through his death and resurrection. This same dynamic is shared by the nations!

The nations experience judgment too, also followed by salvation mediated through the servant of the God of Israel.[12]

First comes judgment.

Judgment of the Nations

The theme of destruction of the nations runs through the Old Testament. God's justice demands that sin and evil be dealt with, but what we find twists our human logic. Judgment is not an end. It is always a means for God to bring all to salvation.

Let's go over Isaiah 45 again since it presents a clear post-judgment salvation for the nations.

> [20] "Gather together and come;
> assemble, you fugitives from the nations.
> Ignorant are those who carry about idols of wood,
> who pray to gods that cannot save.
> [21] Declare what is to be, present it—
> let them take counsel together.
> Who foretold this long ago,
> who declared it from the distant past?
> Was it not I, the LORD?
> And there is no God apart from Me,
> a righteous God and a Savior;
> there is none but Me.

---

[12] I have been and am indebted to Dr. Robin Parry for the following material. Although a good portion of my own research over the past 35 years has already lead me in this same direction. But Dr. Parry's work is impeccable.

> ²² "Turn to Me and be saved,
> all you ends of the earth;
> for I am God, and there is no other.
> ²³ *By myself I have sworn,*
> My mouth has uttered in all integrity
> a word that will not be revoked:
> Before Me every knee will bow;
> by Me *every tongue will swear.*
> ²⁴ *They will say of me, 'In the LORD* alone
> are deliverance and strength.'"
> All who have raged against Him
> will come to Him and be put to shame.
> ²⁵ But all the descendants of Israel
> will find deliverance in the LORD
> and will make their boast in Him. (Isaiah 45:20–25)

Here, the God of Israel addresses the fugitives from the nations. He speaks to Babylonians who have experienced divine judgment. These people are clearly idolaters who pray to gods who cannot save! So the God of Israel calls them to turn to Him—the only God who can save!

What is the nature of this salvation? Is it the same thing as the salvation of Israel? Context shows that this is in fact the case. The exact same Hebrew verb is used in the exact same tense [Niph'al] with reference to Israel just a few verses earlier!

> ¹⁷ But *Israel will be saved* by the LORD
> with an everlasting salvation;
> you will never be put to shame or disgraced,
> to ages everlasting. (Isaiah 45:17)

The salvation of the nations is placed in direct parallel with the salvation of Israel. Whatever it means for Israel to be saved holds true for the nations.

The context is clearly about salvation! It is in this specific context that God swears an oath that every knee bows and every tongue confesses that the God of Israel is the only true God that can save.

But is this a forced submission?

It can't be for a couple of reasons. First of all, we are told that God has called the nations to turn and be saved the same way He saved Israel! Next, we read of mutual oaths. God swears that every knee will bend, and the nations swear that the God of Israel alone can save! Swearing oaths about God is something only someone who intimately knows God can truthfully do!

God declared war on an indwelling evil with the purpose of restoration and liberation of the peoples, and God makes an oath (promise) that He will prevail: the whole world, even those who oppose God, will bow in salvation and declare the deliverance they have experienced.

I think I have written myself happy yet again.

Let's look at a popular objection at this point. Some point out that this passage speaks of some who come to God and are put to shame and insist this means they have not accepted salvation. That being put to shame means they are not saved, but remain lost!

It doesn't logically follow that to come to God and be put to shame means that salvation has been rejected. That notion imposes something into the text that is not there. All the text says is this: when those who raged against God turn to God for salvation, they come in shame because they were opposed to the One whose desire is to save them!

This is reinforced when we compare this passage to Ezekiel 16 which also addresses the Babylonian captives. In this chapter, God speaks to the Israel in bondage and tells them that in spite of repeated idolatry, He will still save them, and as a result, they too will respond in shame (See Ezekiel 16:63). Being ashamed of past idolatry is an appropriate response for those God has redeemed from such things.

We must not overlook the power of God's oath in this passage. Some seem to think that God's oath only reflects a possible future. This conclusion is to ignore the way God's oaths are said to function in Isaiah. We are told that they last forever (40:8) and never return to God without achieving His intent (55:10–11). Universal worship is guaranteed if this is true. Yes, we have read that the nations respond positively to God's call to salvation.

The Bible is filled with many examples of destruction followed by salvation!

Another classic example is found in Isaiah 19. In this chapter, we read of the salvation of Israel's enemies: Egypt and Assyria. The passage is divided into two sections: Egypt's punishment and their subsequent salvation. Judgment unto salvation!

We are told that the Lord rides on a swift cloud (obviously metaphor!) and comes to wage, not just with the Egyptian people, but with the "idols of Egypt [that] tremble before him" (Isaiah 19:1). As the God of Israel comes against Egypt, they will consult their evil "idols and the spirits of the dead" in vain—their plans come to nothing (Isaiah 19:3). It really looks like God has it in for the nation of Egypt, but a closer look reveals something different.

God lifts up His hand to strike Egypt:

> [16] They will shudder with fear at the uplifted hand that the LORD Almighty raises against them ... because of what the LORD Almighty is planning against them. (Isaiah 19:16)

It looks like its curtains, "the end" for Egypt, but:

> ¹⁸ In that day five cities in Egypt will speak the language of
> Canaan and *swear allegiance to the LORD* Almighty ... In
> that day there will be an altar to the Lord in the heart of
> Egypt. (Isaiah 19:18, 19)

What? Allegiance being sworn to Yahweh as a result of God's mighty war against evil? So what has been eliminated in this war? It is the spiritual powers of evil in the gods of Egypt and the evil within them.

The war of God against evil, the judgement and wrath of God against Egypt results in restoration—just like it does for Israel! God is acting against evil—the true evil—evil as a spiritual power that dominates the lives of human beings. God makes war to set mankind free!

When all havoc breaks loose as Egypt is handed over by God to oppressors (Isaiah 19:4), they will repent and turn to the God of Israel and:

> ²⁰ When they cry out to the LORD because of their
> oppressors, He will send them *a savior* and defender, and He
> will *rescue them.* ²¹ So the LORD will make Himself known
> to the Egyptians, and in that day *they will acknowledge the
> LORD. They will worship* with sacrifices and grain offerings;
> they will make vows to the LORD and keep them. ²² *The
> LORD will strike Egypt* with a plague; He will strike them
> *and heal them. They will turn to the LORD*, and He will
> respond to their pleas *and heal them*. (Isaiah 19:20–22)

That passage leaves me breathless! What more can I possibly say?

Take special note of the metaphors throughout this passage. We are told that God will strike the Egyptians, and in 19:4 we find out exactly what that consists of—they are handed over to their enemies.

I can't emphasize this enough—look beyond the retributive, aggressive metaphors used to the restorative end in view.

This passage is prophesying that Egypt will turn to the Saviour, who will rescue them from evil, **after** God declares war on the evil in their nation and makes a judgment against them! Friend, this surely happens!

More of the repeating pattern: judgment first, then salvation! This is the Biblical model!

What God has planned for Egypt is not just for them. Egypt will share this same destiny with all the nations. The very next verse explains this further.

Isaiah addresses the next enemy of Israel: Assyria. God has specifically chosen to target the specific powers that took His chosen people captive. He has put His finger on the world's most evil nations to declare war on evil within and to rescue them from it and set them free! God ultimately responds to all evil with good and prevails in this way.

> [23] *In that day* there will be *a highway from Egypt to Assyria.* The Assyrians will go to Egypt and the Egyptians to Assyria. The Egyptians and Assyrians will *worship together.* [24] *In that day Israel will be the third*, along with Egypt and Assyria, *a blessing on the earth.* [25] The LORD *Almighty will bless them*, saying, *"Blessed be Egypt* my people, *Assyria* my handiwork, and *Israel* my inheritance."
> (Isaiah 19:23–25)

Egypt and Assyria [the arch-enemies of Israel] will worship in unity with Israel! Wow! These oppressive world powers will be healed and restored and together with Israel, will be blessed and be a blessing.

Glory of glories! Can you see Genesis 12:3 coming to fulfilment here? God is recreating the world to bless all the offspring of Adam, including the "wandering nations" that descended from Noah's three boys. The nations at the time of Babel rebelled against the fulfilment of God's blessing, but God intervened with judgment with the goal of restoration and getting them back on track. Then God calls Abraham so that through him the work of blessing all would continue: "Through you and your seed I will bless all nations"! And then we see it playing out! God is carrying out His universal restorative blessing through warfare! What a use of metaphors! God has targeted evil and has declared war on it with plans restore the nations, which are all His offspring, by sending a saviour and leading all to that ONE who will rescue them.

Isaiah blends the promise to bless the nations with a declaration of war on the nations. The purpose of God's warfare on the nations is to cleanse them of evil in preparation for the blessing!

I can't contain myself I have to jump forward. What exactly is this blessing?

> [8] Scripture foresaw that **God would justify the Gentiles by faith**, and announced the **gospel in advance to Abraham**: "**All nations will be blessed** through you." (Galatians 3:8)

Hallelujah! All the nations will accept the Gospel! The blessing promised through the Seed of Abraham is nothing less than the Gospel of justification by faith. All nations will be brought to positively respond to Christ Jesus.

Let me ask you an important question right here right now. Most who have ever lived Egypt and Assyria have died without coming to understand, experience or live by the faith of Christ. So how is it that they all will worship God? The Gospel is preached to the dead (1 Peter

4:5–6). How else can they bow their knee to Jesus unless they hear the Gospel proclaimed to Abraham in a convincing way?

Let me make a very important point here. We have just examined the prophecy that God will save Egypt and Assyria after He has judged them. But when we read of God's judgments on these two nations in Ezekiel 29–32, Nahum and Psalm 139:21—it really looks like these nations are irretrievably lost! Yet, when we put them together with Isaiah 19, we can conclude that even this fierce sounding judgment ends up in salvation! And that is why it is crucial that we piece together the whole unfolding story in the Old Testament!

Judgment is unto salvation for all the nations.

Conclusion

As we step back and look at the forest instead of the trees, we see that the Old Testament as a whole paints a picture of universal salvation of all nations by God through the seed of Abraham. We can see that Israel fails time and time again. She too worships other gods and becomes like the nations needing rescuing. But God knew this and reveals that He has a Servant for His servant–Israel.

Servant–Jesus takes on the identity and role of servant–Israel. He would come and save Israel, taking on their suffering as his own, and as a result, the nations would come streaming to the only true God.

But the Old Testament is mostly all about life on earth, and it doesn't go much further. When the prophets speak about universal salvation, they are talking about everyone alive on earth coming to salvation. Isaiah closes his book with a bizarre picture of a universal salvation of all living human beings—who are looking down on dead bodies! (Isaiah 66:23–24)

The resurrection of Jesus moves us to a different picture of life after death. It is in the New Testament that a more comprehensive universalism is described.

Isaiah presents the idea that every knee will bow down to God and worship him—but these are living beings. Paul takes up this passage of Isaiah 45 and then extends it. He quotes Isaiah in Philippians 2:5–12 saying that "at the name of Jesus every knee will bow and every tongue confess" and adds *"in heaven and on earth and under the earth"*! Amen.

So let's move over and consider how this thread continues to unfold in the New Testament.

CHAPTER FIVE

Jesus Comes as the Nation–Drawing Seed

So far, we have seen that God created mankind for eternal blessing in Eden: "be fruitful and multiply and fill the earth." Adam chose to disobey the instruction of God, to make a decision independent of the source of life, and he died as a result. Mankind came to be in Adam, and so death spread to us all. God's plan never changed. God said to the serpent that the Seed of the woman would crush his head. The Seed is introduced in the very beginning as who would deliver mankind. It would be through the Seed that God would implement His process of restoration—universal restoration! The rest of the Bible tells the story about the Seed who would crush the serpent head and rescue the offspring! Yes judgment is unto salvation!

God put humanity back on track after the flood. To Noah and his three sons, He said: "be fruitful, multiply and fill the earth" (Genesis 9:1–2). Noah heard the same call as the first Adam. Noah's sons obeyed

God and spread over the earth. From them came all the nations—and eventually the Seed (Genesis 10:32).

The nations attempted to come against God's plan of universal restoration once again at Babel. At this time, the nations gathered together in one place to resist God's command to fill the earth (Genesis 11:4). God intervened with a judgment that consisted of confusing their language and spread them across the earth—getting things back on track to all realizing His blessing (Genesis 11:4–8). This Judgment was working towards the salvation of all. It set a pattern. Any attempt to block the universal plan of God is a dead end!

The Bible then shifts focus away from the nations as a whole and towards one man. God promised Abraham that He would continue on to see His plan in the Garden fulfilled through Abraham: "In your *seed all* nations shall be blessed" (Genesis 12:3). The rest of the Bible is about this one verse. Everything in Genesis leads up to this one verse, and the rest of the Bible explains it! The Seed promised to Eve would come through Abraham!

The seed of Abraham was stated to be the nation of Israel. But Israel failed at its calling. Israel, as the seed and the servant, were to draw the nations back to God. After they fail, they learn of the Suffering Servant! This is the Seed who would not only come and rescue Israel, but also draw all nations to God, fulfilling the promise of God.

This is an unfolding story of universal restoration so far. We arrive at the time of the Seed–Servant in the New Testament.

The New Testament tells us that Jesus comes as the Seed–Servant to fulfil the role of national–Israel.

Jesus is as Israel

Matthew 2:15 quotes Hosea 11:1 "Out of Egypt I called my son." In its original context this verse spoke about the nation of Israel and their exodus from Egypt. Matthew applies it to Jesus' escape to Egypt after Herod died. What we will see is that Jesus' life mirrors the story of Israel purposely. Israel passed through the waters of the Red Sea and then entered into a period of testing for 40 years in the wilderness. Jesus passed through the waters of the Jordan in baptism and then was led out into the wilderness to be tested for 40 days! The parallels continue on and on. Jesus has arrived as "God's firstborn."

More to the point is the fact that Jesus is presented as the Servant! The New Testament applies Servant passages from Isaiah directly to Jesus. See Matthew 3:17 cf. Isaiah 42:1; Mark 10:45 cf. Isaiah 53:10; Acts 8:30–35 cf. Isaiah 53:7–8. Jesus has come to fulfil the Servant's mission both to Israel and to the nations!

The Cross is Defined as the Exodus.

> [30] Two men, Moses and Elijah, appeared in glorious splendor, talking with Jesus. [31] They spoke about *his departure*, which he was about to bring to fulfillment at Jerusalem. (Luke 9:30–31)

The Greek word for departure is "exodus"! This is the only place where this word is used in the Gospels, and it is used to refer to the impending crucifixion at Jerusalem. In Christ's death on the cross, Jesus becomes Israel in captivity and exile, and his subsequent resurrection represents Israel's impending release from captivity! Israel is set free! Let's explore this.

We saw in the previous chapter that Isaiah wrote about Israel's Babylonian captivity. They were in exile in Babylon. He promised them that even though they failed their mission as the Servant of the Lord, He would send an individual Servant to be with and as them and rescue them from captivity–exile. Isaiah described the rescue from exile in Babylon as another exodus from Egypt. He blends the current exile in Babylon with their previous captivity in Egypt. A new exodus was on the horizon!

In the same way, the death of Jesus is presented as a new exodus; a release from exile!

So what does that mean? Isaiah tells us that the restoration of all nations would be triggered as a direct result of the witnessing of the exodus–exile–rescue of Israel by the Servant! **This one act of rescue would trigger the pilgrimage of the nations to the God of Israel.** This is significant! Now we can see that Jesus' crucifixion is the exile as well as the beginning of the exodus! The resurrection is the end of the captivity of Israel. *It is this event which triggers the fulfilment of the prophecies regarding the salvation of all.*

The blessing through Abraham to the nations has now been revealed and released through the Seed–Servant—through his death and resurrection.

With this in mind, notice again how Paul deals with the promise given to Abraham.

> [8] Scripture foresaw that God would justify the Gentiles by faith, and announced the gospel in advance to Abraham: "All nations will be blessed through you." (Galatians 3:8)

Paul makes a clear connection between the Gospel and the promise to Abraham! The Gospel is in fact the promise to bless all through Jesus, which he describes as "justification by faith"! This is a very significant application.

Paul even says this:

> [16] The promises were spoken to Abraham and to his seed.
> Scripture does not say "and to seeds," meaning many people,
> but "and to your seed," meaning one person, who is Christ.
> (Galatians 3:16)

The universal blessing of all nations, which for Paul is the Gospel,
comes through the Seed of Abraham—Jesus! These promises were
spoken to Jesus, who has clearly replaced the priesthood of Israel in
Paul's thinking.

And this:

> [29] If you belong to Christ, then you are Abraham's seed, and
> heirs according to the promise. (Galatians 3:29)

We too are the seed of Abraham and heirs if we are in Christ.

Paul states that the Cross was the curse of the law!

What was "the" curse of the law? The supreme curse of the law of
Deuteronomy 28 was exile! Read the whole chapter and notice how
exile is the ultimate curse. It is the final and most devastating curse!
Paul goes on:

> [13] Christ redeemed us from the curse of the law by becoming
> a curse for us, for it is written: "Cursed is everyone who is
> hung on a pole." (Galatians 3:13)

Paul is telling us that Jesus experienced Israel's exile [the curse] when
he hung on the Cross. He relates the curse of exile as the curse found
in Deuteronomy 21.

> [23] You must not leave the body hanging on the pole
> overnight. Be sure to bury it that same day, because **anyone**

who is hung on a pole is under God's curse. (Deuteronomy 21:23)

So hanging on a pole overnight is to be under a curse. But Paul calls it *the* curse! Now did you notice what Paul left out? Deuteronomy clearly says that hanging on a pole or tree is to come under the curse from God! Paul left out the part that says "God's" curse! He never says that God cursed Jesus! Paul frequently edits the Old Testament to deliberately leave out such notions.

More to the point is the fact that Paul has combined the curse of exile with the Cross! *The Cross represents Israel's ultimate exile.* Jesus became the curse—exiled. The Cross also shows that there is a way out of the exile. Jesus—who is the resurrection is that release!

Jesus becomes Israel's exile on the Cross and through his work—they will be brought back!

So notice what Paul says next!

> [13] Christ redeemed us from the curse of the law by becoming a curse for us, for it is written: "Cursed is everyone who is hung on a pole."
> [14] He redeemed us from the curse *in order that the blessing given to Abraham might come to the Gentiles through Christ Jesus*, so that by faith we might receive the promise of the Spirit. (Galatians 3:13–14)

Isaiah has told us that when the nations witness the mighty hand of the God of Israel through His Servant in liberating Israel from the exile—that this mighty act of deliverance would trigger their pilgrimage to Him in fulfilment of the promise of God to bless all nations.

Paul says the same thing here but applies it to the death and resurrection. His death and resurrection represent the exile and the exodus out of captivity. And then Paul tells us that as a result of this ultimate act of release from captivity, the Gentiles are already beginning to experience the blessing given to Abraham—which he has already identified as the Gospel of justification of all the nations by faith!

That is powerful truth!

Isaiah made it clear that when the nations witness the Suffering Servant's works to set Israel free, that this act would release the blessing on all the nations and facilitate the start of their pilgrimage back to God.

Paul calls all this as "done." In his view, the death and resurrection of Jesus means that the exile and release of Israel and the reconciliation of the nations that results have taken place; and so the fulfilment of the blessing of all nations through the Seed of Abraham is also a "done deal"—to be seen and testified throughout the coming ages of exceeding grace. As the nations hear the true gospel message about fulfilled promises, people will call on their Saviour and make their pilgrimage to the true God revealed in Jesus!

What an insight by Paul!

Will **all** actually come to the God revealed through Jesus? We are getting there!

Let me give you a hint: What Jesus has done and achieved and embodied is a foretaste of the literal experiential salvation of Israel and also of all the nations as they flow to God. We will see that although the New Testament speaks of a "now" fulfilment through Jesus, it also describes a "not yet" aspect. It refers to a time when "all

Israel" and the nations experience salvation and worship the God of Israel. Let's move forward.

Jesus not only fulfils the stated role of Israel, but he also undoes the death in Adam!

Jesus the Last Adam

If we consider Jesus as the second and last Adam, we see clear and powerful Universal implications.

Let's use 1 Corinthians 15 as a springboard for this part of our discussion.

> [45] So it is written: "The first man Adam became a living being"; the last Adam, a life-giving spirit. (1 Corinthians 15:45)

Paul makes direct parallels between Jesus and Adam and goes so far as to call Jesus the "last Adam." Jesus is the fountainhead of a new humanity. Adam was a living being, but the last Adam is the source and wellspring of life! How much more Jesus than Adam!

In what specific sense is Jesus the source of life for the human race?

> [20] But Christ has indeed been raised from the dead, the firstfruits of those who have fallen asleep. [21] For since death came through a man, the resurrection of the dead comes also through a man. [22] For as in Adam all die, so in Christ all will be made alive. (1 Corinthians 15:20–22)

Jesus is the firstfruits from the dead of those who have died. Adam brought death to humanity; the last Adam assures us that all who die will be made alive.

Let's address a popular objection: "But it only applies to those in Christ! Only all those in Christ will be made alive." Is this what Paul is asserting here in context? In the first half of this verse Paul says: "IN ADAM all die." He is asserting that we are all in the same boat because of Adam, and this requires no faith at all in Adam. Just as mankind died in and through Adam, this same mankind will live in Christ. Other related texts make this clearer. Paul has placed both statements in deliberate parallel as "just as" statements. To insist that "in Christ" means "those exercising faith in Jesus" would have to mean that "in Adam" means "those exercising faith in Adam" as well. To tamper with either half tampers with the meaning!

The parallelism in context clearly shows that it is the same "all" in both halves of the verse!

This is not to say that I don't believe that people do not need to have personal faith in Jesus. I believe we all do! But I can't let my belief determine Paul's meaning here. In this particular passage, he isn't talking about the faith that we need—his focus is on the first and last Adams!

Just as all die in Adam, so also shall all have life in the Last Adam! All! The "all" discussed doesn't change mid-verse. Paul does not redefine "all" midstream. It's the same all! There is no escaping the conclusion that Jesus as the second and Last Adam brings life to the dead and the dying!

Having said this, let's consider Paul's monumental "universalist" passage in Romans.

> [12] Therefore, just as through one man sin entered the world, and death through sin, and thus death spread to all men, because all sinned— [13] (For until the law sin was in the world, but sin is not imputed when there is no law. [14]

Nevertheless death reigned from Adam to Moses, even over those who had not sinned according to the likeness of the transgression of Adam, who is a type of Him who was to come. [15] But the free gift *is* not like the offense. For if by the one man's offense many died, much more the grace of God and the gift by the grace of the one Man, Jesus Christ, abounded to many. [16] And the gift *is* not like *that which came* through the one who sinned. For the judgment *which came* from one *offense resulted* in condemnation, but the free gift *which came* from many offenses *resulted* in justification. [17] For if by the one man's offense death reigned through the one, much more those who receive abundance of grace and of the gift of righteousness will reign in life through the One, Jesus Christ.)

[18] Therefore, as through one man's offense *judgment came* to all men, resulting in condemnation, even so through one Man's righteous act *the free gift came* to all men, resulting in justification of life. [19] For as by one man's disobedience many were made sinners, so also by one Man's obedience many will be made righteous.

[20] Moreover the law entered that the offense might abound. But where sin abounded, grace abounded much more, [21] so that as sin reigned in death, even so grace might reign through righteousness to eternal life through Jesus Christ our Lord. (Romans 5:12–21 NKJV)

Before we look at this passage in detail, please notice the brackets at the beginning of verse 13 and at the end of verse 17. Many translations have these brackets or dashes to indicate a digression from Paul's train of thought. This means that verse 18 completes the thought of verse 12! So let's try putting verse 18 immediately after verse 12.

^{12} Therefore, just as sin entered the world through one man, and death through sin, and in this way death came to all people, because all sinned—

^{18} Consequently, just as one trespass resulted in condemnation for all people, so also one righteous act resulted in justification and life for all people. ^{19} For just as through the disobedience of the one man the many were made sinners, so also through the obedience of the one man the many will be made righteous. (Romans 5:12, 18)

Did you also notice how Paul picks up the thought of verse 12 in verse 18 and then continues on to finish it? "Just as sin … consequently just as one sin …" It seems that verse 18 is indeed completing the thought of verse 12 as the translators suggest, but verse 12 begins with "therefore" which suggests a connection with what went before it! So to understand the full meaning of verses 18–19, we need to understand how verse 12 functions in Romans.

Professor James D. G. Dunn[13] maintains that Romans 5:12–21 is in fact a summary of everything Paul has been saying in the whole book of Romans from 1:18–5:11.

Let's examine this claim. In Romans 1:18–3:20, Paul outlines his idea of the universal nature of sin.

Paul points out that the Gentiles, who have rejected the true God and worship idols, have sinned in 1:18–32. In 2:1–3:9, he speaks to the Jews and says that they are no better off when they point the finger at the Gentiles!

Then in 3:9ff he makes an initial conclusion:

---

[13] James D. G. Dunn, Romans 1–8, WBC, pp. 271–72

⁹ What shall we conclude then? Do we have any advantage? Not at all! For we have already made the charge that Jews and Gentiles alike are **all under the power of sin.** ¹⁰ As it is written:

"There is no one righteous, not even one;

¹⁹ Now we know that whatever the law says, it says to those who are under the law, so that **every mouth may be silenced and the whole world held accountable to God.** (Romans 3:9–10)

Romans 3:23 sums up the whole argument about sin, and then introduces the solution to the sin problem. Notice the summary and continued flow.

²³ **for *all* have sinned** and fall short of the glory of God, ²⁴ **and *all* are justified** freely by His grace through the redemption that came by Christ Jesus. (Romans 3:23–24)

Did you see what Paul did here in Chapter Three? He made a conclusion about everything he had been saying about the universal nature of sin and then introduces the universal nature of salvation! "All have sinned … and all are justified freely by His grace!" The same all that have sinned are also justified freely by grace: the parallels are deliberate and stunning!

Up to this point, Paul has introduced the idea that the whole world is justified [saved, righteous!] freely by His grace. He introduces the idea of all being universally justified by grace, but he doesn't explain it—yet! He does so in Chapter Five!

In other words, Paul has focused solely on the universality of sin in Romans 1:8–3:23. Then in 3:24, he introduces God's solution in the same universal terms: "all have sinned and all are justified" This is the same all! Then he picks up this thought again and develops it in Romans 5:12–21!

Keep in mind that "*all* have *sinned*" and note the way Romans 5:12 and 18 flow:

> [12] Therefore, just as sin entered the world through one man, and death through sin, and in this way death came to *all people*, because *all sinned*— ...

> [18] Consequently, just as one trespass resulted in condemnation for *all people*, so also one righteous act resulted in justification and life for *all people*. (Romans 5:12, 18)

In Romans 5:12–21 Paul is explaining 3:24 in greater detail. He has said "and all are justified freely by His grace" and now in 5:12–21, he explains this in greater depth. His burden is to show that Christ's one act of righteousness is as wide as sin's corruption in that it reaches the exact same "all."

In showing just how all encompassing the work of Christ is, Paul draws deliberate parallels between the two Adams again. From the first Adam "the many" [Hebrew figure of speech[14] that means all here, as we shall see] died, but from the last Adam "the many" receive and overflowing of God's grace (5:15). Judgment followed sin and brought condemnation from the first Adam, but the gift brought justification [restoration] from the last Adam (5:16). Death reigned through the first Adam but life from the last Adam (5:17). One sin from the first Adam brought condemnation for *all* people and one act of righteousness from the last Adam brought justification [restoration] and life *for all* (5:18). Through the disobedience of the

---

[14] Joachim Jeremias, "*polloi*" in TDNT 6:536–45

first Adam "the many" were made sinners and through the obedience of the Last Adam "the many" will be made righteous (5:19).

Here's the point: Christ's one act of obedience totally reverses the results of Adam's act of disobedience for all!

What is significant for me is the universal RESULTS of what Adam and Jesus did!

> [18] Consequently, just as *one trespass resulted* in condemnation for *all people*, so also *one righteous act resulted* in justification and life for *all people*. (Romans 5:18)

Did Adam's one sin result in a potential death and condemnation for all people? Or was Paul suggesting that death and condemnation were a reality for all through Adam? We can see that he clearly thinks all were affected! In the same way, the one act of Jesus totally results in justification and life for all people! It's the exact same all!

Paul is saying that the solution actually extends as far or further than the problem. Paul asserts repeatedly: "how much more Jesus than Adam" in this chapter. If the solution doesn't reach as far as the problem, then Paul is very confused! He should have said "how much more Adam than Jesus" given Adam impacted all with death with his act, but Jesus only impacted some with Life with his act!

The very same "all people" who were made sinners by Adam are the very same "all people" who will be made righteous! Don't let the phrase "the many" put you off. Paul has made it abundantly clear that all have sinned in Adam which here is described as "the many"! If "the many" who were made sinners through Adam's one sin means "all peoples" then "the many" who will be made righteous means "all peoples" too! To say the "many" is referring to "all" in one verse and not the other is to tamper the verse; Paul purposely puts the statements together to show he is talking about the same people.

Did you notice that Paul did not say that it was only just a possibility that these "many" are made righteous? Paul asserts that they "will"!! He is proclaiming it as a done deal; this is the end result of the work of God through Christ Jesus! All will come to faith because righteousness comes to us only through faith—and all will be made righteous!

Verse 18 states that the same all that were condemned through Adam are also "justified" and have "life" by what Jesus has done! What does he mean by "life"? He can't be talking about human life because we are already alive! So what does he mean by life?

> [18] Consequently, just as one trespass resulted in condemnation for all people, so also one righteous act *resulted in justification and life for all people.*

> [21] so that, just as sin reigned in death, so also grace might reign through righteousness **to bring** *eternal life* **through Jesus** Christ our Lord. (Romans 5:18, 21)

Thank you Jesus! Jesus brought justification and eternal life for all people. All have eternal life waiting to be realized subjectively!

Let's consider some common objections at this point. Again and again, people refer me to verse 17 and point out that the only ones that have life are those who "receive" it! I agree! But Paul says that all will one day believe and receive! The objective finished universal work of Jesus will be subjectively received by all through faith! Paul makes this very point later on in chapters 9–11!

At this time, I do want to say something about the participle "receive" in verse 17. Those who reject universal salvation say that the word "receive" means that it is only those who *actively take* eternal life for themselves by their faith that obtain it. One huge problem with this assertion is that the participle used here is passive, and as such, it is not describing something people are actively doing but something people are passively receiving. For example, I can say "I received a punch on the nose the other day." This does not describe anything active I did but what I received from another. The gift of righteousness I receive is what is being done to me, not by me.

Here we have an example of the word usage from earlier in Romans:

> 5 Through Him we have received grace and apostleship (Romans 1:5 NKJV)

Is Paul saying that grace and apostleship was "received" by him by something he did or that it was conferred upon him?

To receive doesn't necessarily mean that it is something that we actively do by faith. Receive in Romans means something done to me and not "of me"— because it is all a gift.

Look at the way Paul uses the word "receive" earlier in Chapter 5.

The exact same thing is happening in this verse.

> 10 For if, while we were God's enemies, **we were reconciled to him through the death of His Son**, how much more, having been reconciled …
>
> ...through whom we have now *received* reconciliation. (Romans 5:10–11)

When did he say we were we reconciled to God? When Jesus died! In other words, he is saying we "received" reconciliation through the death of His Son, and not when we believed, but while we were enemies! Paul is simply telling us of all the great things we passively receive from God: justification, life, peace!

We received reconciliation when Jesus died on the Cross and not when we did something. In this chapter, receiving is consistently described as passive on our part; it is what is done to us! We passively receive the results of what Jesus has done!

Let's consider another objection—and this one has serious merit. Some insist that although the same "all" is the same group with reference to Adam and Jesus—that this doesn't mean every single human being. The "all" is all kinds of people—Jews and Gentiles in general but not every single human being! But what then are we to make of Paul's statement that "all have sinned"? Does this mean that all kinds of people from Jewish and Gentile backgrounds have sinned but not every single individual?

In fact in Romans 3:9ff Paul explicitly states that every single human being has sinned—and that every single human being is justified:

> [9] ...Jews and Gentiles alike are *all under the power of sin*.
> [10] As it is written: "There is no one righteous, *not even one*;
> (Romans 3:9–10)

Not even one from all the classes or groups of people!

Having made the explicit point that every single person is under the power of sin, Paul concludes:

> [23] for *all have sinned* and fall short of the glory of God, [24] and *all are justified* freely by His grace through the redemption that came by Christ Jesus. (Romans 3:23–24)

All have sinned in Paul's eyes—all people without exception is what he is asserting, and he also asserts that this same all are justified by Jesus!

Some assert that Romans 5:18 only speaks about an offer of justification and eternal life. That it is describing God's desire to save all and nothing more. One problem: Paul doesn't describe it as an offer! He asserts this a definite result of God's work—not as an offer people may or may not take.

> [18] Consequently, just as one trespass *resulted* in condemnation for all people, so also one righteous act *resulted* in justification and life for all people. (Romans 5:18)

One sin *resulted* in condemnation for all and one righteous act *resulted* in justification and eternal life for all. It is not stated as a mere wish that might not be—but as a fact.

Let's focus on what Paul says in his letter to the Philippians.

> [8] And being found in appearance as a man,
> he humbled himself
> by becoming obedient to death—
> even death on a cross!
>
> [9] Therefore God exalted him to the highest place
> and gave him the name that is above every name,
> [10] that at the name of Jesus every knee should bow,
> in heaven and on earth and under the earth,
> [11] and every tongue acknowledge that Jesus Christ is Lord,
> to the glory of God the Father. (Philippians 2:9–12)

Every knee in heaven and earth and even *under* the earth will proclaim that Jesus is Lord.

In this passage, Paul quotes Isaiah 45.

> [21]And there is no God apart from me,
> a righteous God and a Savior;
> there is none but me.
>
> [22] "Turn to me and be saved,
> *all you ends of the earth;*
> for I am God, and there is no other.
> [23] *By myself I have sworn,*
> my mouth has uttered in all integrity
> a word that will not be revoked:
> Before me every knee will bow;
> by me *every tongue will swear.*
> [24] *They will say of me, 'In the LORD* alone
> are deliverance and strength.'"
> All who have raged against him
> will come to him and be put to shame.
> [25] But all the descendants of Israel
> will find deliverance in the LORD
> and will make their boast in him. (Isaiah 45:21–25)

Isaiah says that every living knee would bend to God. Paul quotes Isaiah and says that every dead knee would bend too! This speaks to a post-death experience in which people can be brought to God!

Most accept that this is what Paul is suggesting; but what does Paul mean? Does he mean that every human being that has ever existed will be saved?

Does this mean that all will eventually be saved?

Some insist that this verse is simply saying that at some time in history that the whole universe will acknowledge the Lordship of Jesus. This will include the saved and the lost. For the lost, this will be a forced submission before being cast into hell or while in hell.

Those who hold this view try and support it by saying that Isaiah speaks about those bowing the knee in "shame" which they think means that they have not accepted salvation. They also point out that Romans 14:11 quotes this same passage in Isaiah in the context of appearing before Jesus in a condemnatory judgment!

We have already addressed the passage in Isaiah speaking of the nations bending the knee and that some doing so brought to shame. It doesn't logically follow that to come to God and be ashamed means that salvation is being rejected. That is to impose something into the text that is not there.

What about the way Paul quotes Isaiah 45 in Romans 14 in a judgment context? Surely this means that Isaiah didn't have the salvation of all in mind!

Let's look at Romans 14:11–12 in the context of the whole chapter.

First the verses in question.

> [11] It is written:
> "'As surely as I live,' says the Lord,
> 'every knee will bow before me;
> every tongue will acknowledge God.'"
>
> [12] So then, each of us will give an account of ourselves to God. (Romans 14:11–12)

To be sure, Paul is quoting Isaiah 45 in a judgment context, but where is a judgment unto condemnation? This is read into the text based on the assumption that judgment is about damnation!

Let's examine these verses in the unfolding logic of the chapter as a whole.

Paul is dealing with strife within the church at Rome. They were "quarrelling over disputable matters" (14:1.) The whole book of Romans addresses friction between Jewish and Gentile believers. Strong believers were looking down with contempt at their weaker brothers, and the weaker believers were judging the strong—and all this over non-essentials! (14:1–3). Paul emphasises that each believer is accountable to God on these issues and so should not take on God's role as judge if it divides the body of Christ! (14:4).

It is in this specific context that Paul quotes the divine oath of Isaiah 45 where God vows that all knees will bow to him. The vow of Isaiah 45 serves two purposes. First, Paul quotes Isaiah to stress the point that it is to God that all will eventually bow and so they should not usurp the role of God in this regard, trying to get others to bow to their own individual viewpoints on these matters! Secondly, Isaiah 45 speaks about the salvation of the Gentiles—"turn to me all the world and be saved"—and has them all bowing down *in salvation* alongside the Jews! This is very handy for Paul given he was addressing Jews and Gentiles at Rome that were not getting along! Paul tells them that they are all on equal footing before God! Both groups of "saved believers" will one day appear before God. There is no hint at all of condemnation in this chapter! Paul uses the divine oath of Isaiah 45 simply as a springboard to call Jews and Gentiles to live in harmony!

We have already seen that Isaiah speaks of every Gentile knee bowing in the context of salvation. In fact, he says that they swear that only in the God of Israel is deliverance found!

So in Philippians 2, Paul is quoting a passage that clearly refers to universal salvation; not forced submission of the unsaved! But Paul takes us further than Isaiah. All creatures in heaven and earth, human and angelic, confess that Jesus is Lord to God's glory! Elsewhere Paul says that it is only believers that can make this proclamation that glorifies God—and this only through the indwelling Spirit! (1 Corinthians 12:3). Paul states that whoever truthfully confesses that Jesus is Lord (which can only be done by the Spirit) will be saved! (Romans 10:9–13).

Paul has told us that Jesus has saved Israel as Israel, and that he has saved humanity as Adam. But Paul goes even further than this. We have read that every knee in *heaven* and earth will bow to Jesus and declare his Lordship.

What happened on the Cross even results in cosmic reconciliation.

Cosmic Reconciliation

Every knee in heaven will also declare that Jesus is Lord. Paul takes this up in Colossians.

> [15] Christ is the visible image of the invisible God. He existed before anything was created and is supreme over all creation,

> [16] For through him God created *everything in the heavenly realms and on earth. He made the things we can see and the things we can't see—* such as thrones, kingdoms, *rulers, and authorities* in the unseen world. Everything was created through him and for him.

> [20] and through him God *reconciled everything to himself.* He *made peace* with *everything in heaven and on earth* by means of *Christ's blood on the cross.*(Colossians 1:15–16, 20 NLT)

Paul speaks of the creation of heavenly and earthly realms, the fall of both, and their reconciliation—and this is through blood shed on the Cross.

Paul has just furnished us with a meta-narrative; the storyline of the whole Bible. Creation, the fall, and recreation!

And he tells us in no uncertain terms that all things in both realms whether they are human on invisible rulers and authorities have already been reconciled. The death of Jesus has cosmic overtones. The same "all things" that were created and fell—these same "all things" have been reconciled to God at the Cross through the blood! This includes heavenly beings as well.

Paul takes this up also in Ephesians 1.

> [9] He made known to us the mystery of His will according to His good pleasure, which He purposed in Christ, [10] to be put into effect when the times reach their fulfilment—to bring unity to all things in heaven and on earth under Christ. (Ephesians 1:9–11)

Did you notice that God's mystery was about what He purposed in Christ? At the right time, God set into motion the plan to bring to unity "all things" in heaven and on earth under Christ Jesus! Clearly, some things in heaven were not in unity, just as on earth! But that is also resolved!

Conclusion

In this chapter, we considered how the New Testament speaks of Jesus both as Israel and the last Adam.

As Israel, Jesus takes upon himself the curse of the law, the exile, the hanging on a tree. In his resurrection, he demonstrates an exodus out of exile into freedom and new life, which is the salvation of the Lord. We saw that this act of deliverance by the Seed of Abraham, the Servant of God, also triggers the salvation of the Gentiles!

As the last Adam, Jesus undoes the curse of the first Adam; in this, he represents the whole human family—not just Israel. In Adam, all humanity dies; in the last Adam, all humanity lives.

With the coming of Jesus and Pentecost, we see that some Jews and Gentiles do indeed bow the knee to Jesus. The book of Acts tells us that it was Israel that came to Jesus first as a result of his death and resurrection. The rest of the book of Acts describes the way this restoration of Israel became the trigger to take the Gospel of restoration to all the nations! The prophecy of Isaiah was being fulfilled then already, but not completely. This is a foretaste of what is yet to come.

In the following chapters, I will show how Romans 9–11 and Revelation 14–22 describe an end–time fulfilment when "all Israel" will be saved which then triggers the pilgrimage of "all the nations" to the Temple to worship the God of Israel revealed in Jesus!

Let's consider what Paul says about this in Romans 9–11 where he deals with Israel!

CHAPTER SIX

Universal Salvation in Romans 9–11[15]

So far we have seen that God had chosen Israel to bring the truth about their God to the nations. In a sense Israel was called in Old Testament times to preach the Gospel to the nations! As the seed of Abraham and the Servant of God they failed their mission so God sent another Servant, the Seed, to identify with Israel, embody Israel, endure Israel's exile on the Cross and liberate them through his resurrection. This should have resulted in the evangelisation of all nations. But, Jesus the Seed–Servant came and the nation Israel rejected their Messiah–Saviour—the Gospel. It really seemed that God's word to Abraham in some sense had failed!

This raised serious questions about God's faithfulness to His promises in this whole plan and so Paul dedicates three whole chapters to deal

---

[15] I am indebted to Dr Robin Parry, Evangelical Universalist, Dr James D. G. Dunn, The Theology of Paul, for many of the ideas in this chapter

with this issue. Remember that God's faithfulness to His word is what the Gospel is about and so this issue needs to be dealt with head on given it places question on the very Gospel itself.

Early in Romans Paul introduces the idea that Israel had rejected God.

> [1]What advantage, then, is there in being a Jew, or what value is there in circumcision? [2]Much in every way! First of all, the Jews have been entrusted with the very words of God. [3]What if some were unfaithful? ***Will their unfaithfulness nullify God's faithfulness?*** [4]Not at all! (Romans 3:1–4)

Israel[16] was entrusted with the words of God but she failed. This could be seen as placing serious doubt on God's faithfulness to His word to Abraham.

Paul picks up this idea in detail in Chapters 9–11. Paul will be careful to tell us in these chapters that God is faithful to Israel and His promises to them, even though Israel rejected Jesus!

> [28]As far as the gospel is concerned, they [Jews that rejected Jesus] are enemies for your sake; but as far as election is concerned, they are loved on account of the **patriarchs,** [29]**for God's gifts** and His call are irrevocable. (Romans 11:28–29)

Paul sees that the promise, the gifts and the call made to the patriarchs were in the process of being fulfilled. We need to take special note of the way Paul explains how it was all being realised.

---

[16] Dunn makes a distinction between Jew and Israelite which I will not engage. I agree with him that we need to make a distinction between a "Jew" and an "Israelite." See Theology of Paul, 499–532.

In these chapters Paul explains to us exactly how the promise made to Abraham to bless all nations through his seed, will come to pass now that Jesus has come and ascended to heaven. Paul will explain it in terms of a "mystery" that was playing out! (Romans 11:25–26). Everything was happening on time and in the exact way God had planned it. In other words God's word had not failed. Let's see how Paul unpacks all of this.

An Overview

In this chapter I will demonstrate that God's plan to bless and save all nations through the seed of Abraham was in the process of coming to pass. Paul deals with many issues in these three chapters but I will focus on what is relevant to universal salvation.

Paul begins his discussion by defining what an Israelite actually is. Once we know that then we can see that God's word had not failed. He defines an Israelite in terms of God's *call* and election. God determines who an Israelite is; it's a matter of grace and not human effort through physical descent and procreation. Those called had in fact accepted Jesus so in this sense God's word did not fail! Once Paul settles this issue he then moves forward to tell us that God had shown him a "mystery" about the way God intended to save to whole human race!

In Chapter 11 of Romans, Paul outlines a brief scenario; God's strategy to bring all humanity to salvation. He begins by telling us that a remnant of Jews in his day had accepted Jesus—whilst the rest were hardened by God! As strange as this sounds to us, we learn that this was a temporary condition which had a specific goal in mind—the salvation of the world! This temporary hardening caused the focus of the Gospel to go out to the Gentiles during the Christian era. But not all the Gentiles will be saved during this period. Growing numbers of

Gentiles would experience the blessing of Abraham whilst the unbelieving Jews who were hardened would not. This would serve to provoke Israel to jealousy and so prepare them for what was about to come.

Paul speaks of a time when the "fullness" of the Gentiles finally arrives. This is not all the Gentiles—the nations—not yet anyway!

This fullness of the Gentiles, the coming in of the nations, does its work: Israel will be provoked to jealousy and so comes to faith—all of them are saved—when Jesus returns from heaven. It is only after "all Israel" is saved and restored that the promise to Abraham comes to complete fulfilment. This end-time restoration of Israel then triggers the pilgrimage of all the remaining nations–Gentiles to Jesus *after* Jesus has already returned to earth. And in this way the promise to Abraham is fulfilled in full.

So let's follow Paul's intricate logic throughout these three chapters and tease out this strategy.

Did God's Word fail? In anguish Paul tells us that his heart is torn because his people had rejected Jesus. But he can still affirm that they are still the people of God nonetheless!

> [4] Theirs *is* the adoption to sonship … and *the promises.* [5]
> Theirs *are* the patriarchs, and from them is traced the human
> ancestry of the Messiah, who is God over all, forever
> praised! Amen. (Romans 9:4)

So there is no doubt that although Paul feels torn about the *current* state of Israel, yet he can assert that they are *still* the people of God— that theirs *are,* present tense, the *promises* made to Abraham!

In the next three chapters Paul begins to explain this paradox: they are currently in a lost state but still are the people of God and still have the promises! See also 11:28–29.

Paul raises the question and answers it immediately:

> [6] It is not as though God's word had failed. For not all who are descended from Israel are Israel. [7] Nor because they are his descendants are they all Abraham's children. On the contrary, "It is through Isaac that your offspring will be reckoned." [8] In other words, it is not the children by *physical descent* who are God's children, but it is the children of *the promise* who are regarded as Abraham's offspring. (Romans 9:6–8)

Paul begins his argument in Romans 9 by asking the obvious question: "Did God's word fail"? Paul answers this question and will tell us that the problem is not that God's word failed Israel—the real issue is our failure to understand who Israel really is! He will spend the whole of this chapter defining Israel to emphasise that God's word had not failed Israel at all and that God's word was being fulfilled on time.

Israel is not ethnic Israel of natural physical descent; as was commonly believed in the first century. Israel is those who are arbitrarily "called" by God. Paul will labour this point throughout this chapter since he is demonstrating that God's word to Israel did not fail given Israel was not an ethnic entity.

The key word in Romans 9 is "call."

> [12] Not by works but by Him who *calls*— (Romans 9:12)

> [24] Even us, whom He also *called*, [25] As He says in Hosea:

"I will *call* them 'My people' who are not My people;
and I will *call* her 'My loved one' who is not My loved one,"

[26] there they will be *called* 'children of the living God.'"
(Romans 24–26)

Paul connects "call" directly with his definition of Israel. The true Israelite is the one called, that is, elected by God's sovereign grace. Israel is not defined by physical descent, Israel is the people called by God. It is defined by God's word and promise (9:8), God's election and choice of grace (9:11).

Paul has just confronted the popular definition of Israel of his day and rejected it! He will demonstrate this by telling us that Israel can't be defined simply in terms of physical descent because Abraham had Ishmael by Hagar (and not Sarah his wife) and he was not an Israelite as far as God was concerned. It is only the children like Isaac who are based on God's promise that are the seed of Abraham (9:7–9).

Paul will go even further. Consider the twin boys of Isaac, Abraham's son.

In the case of Ishmael and Isaac it could be argued that two separate mothers were involved. But not so with Isaac's twins: Jacob and Esau! God arbitrarily put His finger on Jacob the second born as the child of promise just to reinforce the idea that election is based solely on God's sovereign call and choice!

> [10] Not only that, but Rebekah's children were conceived at the same time by our father Isaac. [11] Yet, *before the twins were born or had done anything good or bad*—in order that God's purpose in election might stand (Romans 9:10–11)

According to the religious reasoning of the day the blessing should have passed onto the firstborn Esau but Paul makes it clear that the promise is based on God's sovereign call of grace and not human reasoning or effort through human physical descent.

What is striking is the fact that Jacob's election (9:11) took place whilst the twin boys were still in the womb emphasizing the point that election is based solely by the calling of grace and not "from works" (9:10–12).

Paul is so determined to get across the idea that God's promise to save is based solely on grace and His arbitrary choice that he will even go on to tell us by contrast that God at times will even harden some people like Pharaoh (9:14–18). God chooses who will receive mercy and who will not: "Therefore God has mercy on whom He wants to have mercy, and He hardens whom He wants to harden" (9:18). Although this will sound like some are doomed forever, it is not what Paul is really saying for later on in Chapter 11 he will tell us that God hardens temporarily and with the specific purpose of showing mercy to all! But he won't say this yet. He wants to make his point clear: salvation is all of God's grace and election.

Paul will even rub salt in the religious wound and then tell us that God as the potter has full right to do as He wishes with the clay. In this chapter we are told that God has molded two kinds of pots: one for mercy and the other hardened as vessels of wrath (9:22–23).

Paul says all of this to make one point solidly clear:

> [16]So then it ***depends not on human will or exertion***, but on God, who has mercy.

> [18] So then He has mercy on whomever He wills, and He hardens whomever He wills. (Romans 9:16,18 ESV)

We need to keep on track with Paul's main point: Israel is defined by God's call and election based on grace and not human efforts through physical descent.

He says this to answer his initial question: God's word and promise to Israel has not failed. The truth is that we have failed to correctly understand who Israel is. God's word has and was in the process of being fulfilled. Everything was on target.

Paul now takes us into uncharted territory. The Israel of God's call included both Jews and Gentiles.

> 24 Even us, whom He also called, not only from the Jews but also from the Gentiles (Romans 9:24)

The called, chosen and elect also includes the Gentiles! Paul is laying his universal foundation which he will bring out into the open in Chapter 11! What we will find there is that God has arbitrarily called the whole human race—eventually!

In 9:33 Paul begins to shift focus and introduces a most radical idea: Israel as a nation rejected Jesus because God planned it this way.

> 33 As it is written:
> "See, *I lay in Zion a stone that causes people to stumble*
> and a rock that *makes them fall* and the one who believes in
> him will never be put to shame." (Romans 9:33)

We are presented with a tension: on the one hand God causes people to stumble and yet it is still possible to believe in Jesus! Paul will bring this up again in Chapter 10 but it is not until Chapter 11 that he explains in full what he means by this paradox: we will see that he refers to this plan as God's unfolding mystery to save the entire human race.

In Chapter 10 Paul tells us that although Israel had heard the Gospel; she did not come to faith (10:15–18).

Why? He has already made it clear in 9:33 that some do believe and others are caused to stumble by God. God hardens some and others He doesn't! Salvation is solely in God's control; it's about grace not works! So why did Israel not come to faith given they heard?

> [16] But not all the Israelites accepted the good news. For Isaiah says, "Lord, who has believed our message?"
> [17] Consequently, *faith comes from hearing* the message, and the message is heard through the word about Christ.
> [18] But I ask: *Did they not hear? Of course they did:*
>
> "Their voice has gone out into all the earth, their words to the ends of the world."
> [19] Again I ask: Did Israel not understand? First, Moses says, "*I will make you envious* by those who are not a nation;
> (Romans 10:16–19)

Again we read that Israel heard the Gospel but did not come to faith; they stubbornly refused to believe (10:21). But it is not simply a matter of hearing and then choosing to reject Jesus.

Something else behind the scenes was taking place. Israel's rejection of Jesus is directly connected to being provoked to jealousy by the Gentiles when they see them experience the blessing of Abraham— whilst they do not! (10:19).

By talking about Israel being provoked to jealousy Paul is giving us a loud hint as to why Israel failed to believe. This provoking to jealousy is the major theme of Chapter 11.

¹¹ Again I ask: Did they stumble so as to fall beyond recovery? Not at all! Rather, because of their transgression, salvation has come to the Gentiles *to make Israel envious*.

¹⁴ in the hope that I may somehow *arouse my own people to envy and save some of them.*

²⁶ and in this way [by being provoked to salvation envy] all Israel will be saved. (Romans 11:11, 14, 26)

Oh I want to break out into praise at this point! God has a plan that He is control of by which He will save all Israel! Imagine using envy of salvation to get people saved?! Father is in the business of saving all and He keeps eternal destiny fully within His grasp. People will and must believe and it will happen when He has provoked Israel to jealousy—and in the meantime He hardens. I am ahead of myself!

So it is not simply a matter of Israel hearing the Gospel and rejecting it. Other underlying issues were playing out behind the scenes by God where the mystery of universal salvation was unfolding.

Paul will tell us in Chapter 11 that "the called" includes the whole world.

It's as we enter Chapter 11 that we encounter Paul's full blown universal salvation.

Paul starts this chapter by bringing us back to his central thought. "I ask therefore has God rejected His people?" (11:1).

It is only after having defined Israel in terms of God's call of grace that he unravels what he calls the "mystery" (11:25).

This chapter can be outlined as follows:

1. God's word continues to be fulfilled through a remnant within ethnic Israel (11:1–6)

2. The non–remnant part of ethnic Israel was hardened and stumbled into unbelief by divine will with the view to a glorious great plan (11:17–24)

3. God intended to break off some of the natural branches, the hardened, temporarily in order to graft in Gentiles which would provoke the non-remnant hardened Israel to salvation–jealousy (11:17–24)

4. The end result of God's mystery was nothing less than salvation of the entire human race (11:25–32)

Let's unpack this Universalist outline.

Paul speaks about two groups within Israel: the elect and the rest. The elect are those that have accepted Jesus and the "rest" (cf. 11:7) have rejected him by being hardened.

> [7] What then? What *the people of Israel* sought so earnestly they did not obtain. **The elect among them** did, but **the *rest*** were hardened (Romans 11:7)

The people of Israel are made up of two groups: "the elect among them" and "the rest" who he refers to as the hardened. You will remember that Paul had already referred to the hardened back in Chapter 9. He now applies this term directly to Israel with the most marvellous twist!

For now we need to keep this distinction clearly in our minds as we continue on with the rest of the chapter.

God's word continues to be fulfilled through a remnant within ethnic Israel. In Chapter 11 Paul returns to his initial question raised in Chapter 9 and now he will answer it in greater detail: "Well then…

Did God reject His people?" and he replies, "By no means!" (11:1). The rest of the chapter explains what was really happening. First of all, a remnant of the Jews, himself included, had already been chosen *by grace* at the present time.

> [1] I ask then: Did God reject His people? By no means! I am an Israelite myself ... [2] God did not reject His people ... Don't you know what Scripture says in the passage about Elijah ... "I have reserved for myself seven thousand who have not bowed the knee to Baal." [5] So too, *at the present time there is a remnant chosen by grace.* [6] And if by grace, then it *cannot be based on works*; if it were, grace would no longer be grace. (Romans 11:1–6)

God's word has not failed. God had arbitrarily chosen a remnant by grace as He had in Elijah's day: Paul was part of this remnant of Israel chosen by God. We have already seen that Paul refers this remnant of grace as the "elect"! The remnant, the elect, the chosen are all the same group.

Please note the way Paul emphasises his main point: salvation is by grace alone without human effort. This is his axe to grind! He wants to emphasise one point: salvation is in the control of God alone. It is all of grace. God chooses how and when people are saved. To be sure faith is essential. But we need to see how faith works in this whole process. Paul will now come out of his closet. Only a remnant of Israel accepted Jesus and the rest rejected him because God planned it this way!

> [7] What then? What the people of Israel sought so earnestly they did not obtain. The elect among them did, but the *others were hardened,* [8] as it is written:
>
> > *"God gave them a spirit of stupor,*
> > eyes that could not see

and ***ears that could not hear,***
to this very day."(Romans 11:7–8)

Paul has dropped hints along the way that Israel had rejected Jesus for reasons that went beyond human–initiated refusal to believe. Now he spells it out clearly: the others were hardened by God so that they could not see or hear; remember in 10:14–17 he has said that "faith comes by hearing" and now God chose that they could not hear! Things are happening behind the scenes which we have not noticed. God's plan continues on unhindered; His word has not failed at all!

It is about to unfold in the most marvellous universal way! Watch what unfolds now!

It seems that this situation is irreversible. But it is now, at this point that the plot twists. Paul now picks up and elaborates on the hardening of the vessels of wrath mentioned initially in 9:22–23.

> [11] Again I ask: Did they stumble so as to fall beyond recovery? Not at all! Rather, because of their transgression, **salvation has come to the Gentiles to make Israel envious.** [12] But if their transgression means **riches for the world**, and their loss means **riches for the Gentiles**, how much greater riches will **their fullness bring**! (Romans 11:11–12)

The twist! Israel may have been hardened and thus stumbled over the gospel, but this does not place them beyond recovery. Their rejection of Jesus was planned by God all along with the view to saving the Gentiles which functioned to provoke Israel to jealousy! God has been behind the large moves of history bringing about His predetermined will—which we will see is universal salvation! This plan is called the "mystery"(11:25–26). But before we look at these particular verses, note the way Paul continues to develop this idea.

Paul goes on to warn the Gentile Christians not to become smug and so look down on unbelieving Jews in 11:13–24. In these verses Paul tells us that Israel is like an olive tree. Jews who have not believed the gospel have been broken off. This is a way of picturing what Paul means when he says that not all Israel are Israel (9:5). God has been stern with them (11:22), and rejected them (11:15), as vessels of wrath prepared for destruction (9:22–23). Is such a state permanent? Not necessarily: "if they do not persist in unbelief they will be grafted in, for God is able to graft them in again" (11:23). So faith in Jesus is part of this whole process. Yes, Israel was hardened by God, they could not believe, but they can and will eventually according to God's plan. They can and will be grafted back into the elect. This means that the elect is not a rigidly fixed category. It is an open, flexible group. When God calls them they will come to faith and be part of the elect—and this will include the whole human race as we shall soon see!

If the rest that rejected Jesus do not persist in unbelief, they will be re-grafted into the olive tree. But will this condition actually come to pass? Yes.

> [25]I do not want you to be ignorant of this *mystery*, brothers, so that you may not be conceited: Israel has experienced *a hardening in part until the full number of the Gentiles has come in*. [26] And so all Israel will be saved, as it is written: "The deliverer will come from Zion; he will turn godlessness away from Jacob. [27] And this is my covenant with them when I take away their sins." [28] As far as the gospel is concerned, they are enemies on your account; but as far as election is concerned, they are loved on account of the patriarchs, [29] for God's gifts and His call are irrevocable (Romans 11:25–29)

Those who were hardened remained so but only "until"! The situation will come to an end when the full number of the Gentiles comes to salvation. A large part of Israel, the "rest," has been hardened in unbelief for destruction but this was only to enable the gospel to go to the Gentiles. Once the "fullness of the Gentiles has come in" (v. 25), the hardening time will conclude, and then "all Israel will be saved" (11:26). It will be at this time that "the rest," those hardened as vessels of wrath for destruction, become recipients of mercy (11:31). This is another clear example of "judgment unto salvation" that I mentioned earlier in this book.

"All Israel will be saved as it is written: the deliverer will come from Zion"; when the deliverer (Jesus) comes from Zion to earth! At this time the "rest" come to faith; unbelief is dealt with once and for all. Jesus takes away the block: the sin of unbelief!

So has God's word failed? No! God had intended to save them all along. God had decided through His own will to divide Israel into two groups with the view to saving all of them only after the Gospel had first gone out to the nations! To be sure in the interim "the rest," the "broken branches" were hardened and became enemies of the church and the Gospel (11:28), but this did not negate the promise made to Abraham given the promise was *irrevocable* (11:29). God had planned all along to save them all! When Messiah returns, it would be then that "all Israel will be saved" (11:25–28). The temporary condition of unbelief had the salvation of all people in mind.

This also tells us something about the nature of the "destruction" they were experiencing! It simply meant a temporary state of being "not saved"! The Greek word for "destruction" is *apolummi* and in fact its root meaning is to be lost! It is the same basic word translated "lost" in the parable of the "lost" sheep. Destruction simply means temporary "lostness" which comes before being saved!

So God's severity towards the hardened "rest" was only with the intent of showing mercy to all (11:31–32).

It is at this point that Paul breaks out into exuberant praise. God's mystery had been revealed: God had the salvation of the world in mind the whole time. God was in fact behind the scenes guiding history with a view to universal salvation (11:33–36). All things were made by God and for God and would eventually return to God (11:36).

So had God's word failed? By no means! God had chosen a faithful remnant of Israel in Paul's day. The remnant of Israel in the Old Testament always functioned as a promise of future restoration of the whole.[17] This is God's way!

So does Paul really teach universal salvation in Romans 9–11?

Let's consider in greater detail what Paul means by the phrase "all Israel will be saved."

Does this phrase mean that every single Jew will be saved?

Interpreters suggest a number of different ways of understanding what "all Israel will be saved" means.

Some suggest that "all Israel" refers to "spiritual Israel," however, Paul has already listed two distinct groups within Israel: the remnant who accepted Jesus and the rest that rejected him. Paul nowhere refers to a "spiritual Israel" that replaces a literal Israel anywhere in these chapters.

Paul has made it clear that God has a plan for *unbelieving* Israel and that is this: to save them. Paul has told us that God still has a future plan for those broken branches! God intends to unite these two groups together! That is, all Israel will be saved! "All Israel" according to the

---

[17] Genesis 7:23; 2 Kings 19:30–31; Isaiah 11:11–12, 16; 37:31–32; Micah 2:12; 4:7; 5:7–8; Zechariah 8:12

immediate and greater contexts is made up of the believing remnant and the unbelieving majority. "All Israel" means exactly that.

Others say that "all Israel" does not necessarily mean every individual Israelite will be saved. They insist that the whole of Israel does not include each person. Dr. F.F. Bruce in his Tyndale Commentary on Romans, p. 210 asserts that although the language presents a clear Universalism that it is representative rather than individual.

> "There is an unmistakable Universalism in Paul's language here, even if it be an eschatological [end time] Universalism and not a present one, or a representative rather than an individual Universalism."

On this same page he refers to J. Munck and says that a representative Universalism by various individuals of various nations is in view!

Scholars recognize that Paul is clearly using universal language here and so have to deal with his statement: after all it is the punch line of everything he has been saying about Israel so far!

But what is missed is this: Paul is not just talking about the salvation of all Israel but the salvation of all! "God has bound all men over to disobedience so that He may have mercy on them all" (11:32). Paul even says that God's gifts and call to Abraham are irrevocable! God promised Abraham that He would bless His seed and all the nations through the seed and now Paul says it will happen! Everything is on track!

Paul has made it clear back in Chapter 3 that "there is none righteous no not one" and that "all have sinned"! This can only mean every single human being that has ever existed. And then he can say: "all have sinned and all are justified by grace" (Romans 3:23–24). The same "all" that have sinned are also "all justified by grace"! Every single human being is the only interpretation that applies in these verses.

And then there is Romans 5:18, where Paul tells us that every single human being received death and condemnation from Adam and that this very same group has received life and justification from Jesus! This can only mean every single human being, otherwise we can conclude that not all have sinned!

Paul then says the same thing in 11:32: God has bound all to disobedience so that He can show mercy to all! Even our disobedience is part of His plan to have mercy on all! Yes, "all Israel" can only mean every single Israelite according to the greater context of the book as a whole. But more than this, it also includes every single Gentile as well!

I have a feeling that the Western church has problems with this simply because Paul's view of grace was much stronger than ours!

So let's tie all this discussion to the basic thesis: God will restore Israel and then this triggers the pilgrimage of all nations to God.

Is this scenario described in Romans 9–11? On the surface level it looks like the opposite is true: God seems to use the salvation of the Gentiles to provoke Israel to salvation!

But let's look deeper. Consider these pivotal verses where Paul provides us with a brief chronological outline of salvation–events:

> [11] Again I ask: Did they stumble so as to fall beyond recovery? Not at all! Rather, because of *their transgression, salvation has come to the Gentiles* to make Israel envious. [12] But if *their transgression means riches for the world*, and *their loss means riches for the Gentiles*, how *much greater riches will their fullness bring!* (Romans 11:11–12)

Paul makes a number of parallel statements in these verses:

"Because of *their transgression*, **salvation** has come **to the Gentiles**"

"But if *their transgression* means **riches for the world**"

"And *their loss* means **riches for the Gentiles**"

"How **much greater riches** will *their fullness* bring!"

Paul refers to Israel's hardening as their transgression and loss. He tells us that their transgression and loss results in "salvation–riches for the world–Gentiles." In the middle of this he has told us that this whole dynamic serves to trigger Israel to salvation jealousy: "because of their transgression, salvation has come to the Gentiles to make Israel envious." But then he makes the most wonderful contrast. When Israel's envy of the Gentiles salvation results in their salvation then their "loss" will turn to "fullness" and then this "fullness" will bring even greater riches for the Gentiles—which in context means further salvation.

What does Paul mean by Israel's "loss" turning to "fullness"? Well we know for one thing that he has deliberately placed the word "loss" in direct parallel to their current transgression and hardening! We have also been told a number of times that Israel was currently lost.

> [1] Brothers and sisters, my heart's desire and prayer to God for the Israelites is that they *may be saved.*

> [14] In the hope that I may somehow arouse my own people to envy and *save some of them.* (Romans 10:1; 11:14)

Their current loss of salvation will become "fullness" when their salvation envy has done its work. But what does Paul mean by "fullness"—how many Israelites will be "envied" into salvation?

> Israel has experienced a hardening in part until the full number of the Gentiles has come in, [26] and *in this way all Israel will be saved* (Romans 11:25–26)

Paul has made his point: when the full number of Gentiles has come to salvation then Israel will come to faith and be saved; ALL Israel.

We are not told exactly what constitutes the full number of Gentile salvations is but we are told that this number is connected to a very major event!

> [26] and in this way all Israel will be saved. As it is written:

> "*The deliverer will come* from Zion;
> he will turn godlessness away from Jacob.
> [27] And this is my covenant with them
> when I take away their sins." (Romans 11:26–27)

As radical as this sounds, it is nonetheless true. The full number of the Gentiles' salvation ushers in the return of Jesus from heaven. When Jesus returns he will bring all Israel to faith and salvation! What a marvellous scenario!

Jesus said a similar thing:

> [14] And this gospel of the kingdom will be preached in the whole world as a testimony to all *nations*, and then the end will come. (Matthew 24:14)

A time will come when the Gospel has resulted in the full number of Gentiles being saved and this will usher in the end which Matthew tells us is the return of Jesus in glory (Matthew 24:30–31). Jesus said in these verses that the "elect" will be gathered together from the four corners of the earth! Paul tells us that the elect is universal!

So Paul and Jesus agree on this point. But Paul goes further. He tells us that the return of Jesus will bring about the salvation of all Israel when he turns them away from unbelief!

And yet there is more. Paul has also made the point that after Israel is saved when Jesus returns that this will bring with it even greater salvation riches for the Gentiles—and this after the return of Jesus from heavenly Zion!

Paul has provided us with evidence that even more Gentiles will be saved beyond the "full number" and this after the second coming of Jesus.

So here is a basic chronology as Paul describes:

1. God hardens Israel against Jesus, they don't come to faith
2. This allows the focus of the Gospel to be on the Gentiles
3. When the full number of Gentiles are saved Israel is finally provoked by jealousy seeing that the Gentiles are experiencing the blessing of Abraham and they are not
4. Jesus clinches the deal by grace when he returns to deliver Israel and so saves them all
5. This will be followed by even greater salvation riches for the Gentiles after the second coming of Jesus!

How many more Gentiles will be saved after Jesus comes? Does this "greater riches" [salvation in context] for the Gentiles mean universal salvation? Paul does not leave us guessing! The end result is clear:

> [30] Just as you [Gentiles] who were at one time disobedient to God have now received mercy as a result of their [Israel's]

disobedience, [31] so they [Israel] too have now become disobedient in order that they too may now receive mercy as a result of God's mercy to you. [32] For God has bound everyone over to disobedience so that He may *have mercy on them all.* (Romans 11:30–32)

God has bound all over to disobedience at some time or other in order to show mercy on all!

All Israel and all Gentiles will be saved!

When Paul says "may" he means "will."

Look at the way he has used this word in this chapter already to mean "will."

[9] And David says:
"**May** their table become a snare and a trap,
a stumbling block and a retribution for them.
[10] **May** their eyes be darkened so they cannot see,
and their backs be bent forever." (Romans 11:9–10)

and,

[30] Just as you who were at one time disobedient to God have now received mercy as a result of their disobedience, [31] so they too have now become disobedient **in order that they too may now receive mercy** as a result of God's mercy to you. [32] For God has bound everyone over to disobedience so that **He may** have mercy on them all. (Romans 11:30–32)

In verses 7–9 Paul has used the word "may" to mean something definite, not something possible. "God has given them a spirit of stupor so that they may not understand"! Clearly "may" does not mean a possibility but something definite.

Then in the verse just before the one in question Paul has used the word "may" again to mean a certainty! He has already made the point clear that "all Israel WILL be saved" and now in verse 31 he has said the same thing using the word "may": "they too may receive mercy" means "all Israel will be saved"! The word "may" means will and "mercy" can only mean salvation! Yes! Salvation for all!

So there we have it! God saves a remnant of Israel now and hardens the rest temporarily to get salvation out to the Gentiles at the present time. This provokes Israel to jealousy and salvation. When all Israel is saved when Jesus returns, this triggers greater riches of salvation for the nations which means "all" in verses 30–32.

This universal salvation causes Paul to break out in praise as he closes the doctrinal section of the book of Romans.

> Oh, the depth of the riches of the wisdom and knowledge of God! How unsearchable His judgments, and His paths beyond tracing out! "Who has known the mind of the Lord? Or who has been His counselor?" "Who has ever given to God, that God should repay him?" For from him and through him and to him are all things. To him be the glory forever! Amen. (Romans 11:33–36)

Yes indeed. No one could have possibly known what God had in mind! Human eternal destiny is solely in the hands of God through His mystery! The Gospel in Romans is that God will save all who put faith in Jesus (1:14–17). And now we read the way God brings all to faith in Jesus! Amen!

All things came from God and all things will come to him—all will find their eternal destiny in God eventually (11:36).

Paul returns one last time to this theme in Chapter 15. And it is here that he ties all of this together to Genesis 12:3.

⁸ For I tell you that Christ has become a servant of **the Jews** on behalf of God's truth, **so that the promises made to the patriarchs might be confirmed** ⁹ **and**, moreover, **that the Gentiles might glorify God for His mercy**. As it is written:

"Therefore I will praise you among the Gentiles;
I will sing the praises of your name."

¹⁰ Again, it says, "Rejoice, *you Gentiles, with His people.*"

¹¹ And again, "Praise the Lord, *ALL you Gentiles;*
let ALL the peoples extol him."

¹² And again, Isaiah says,
"The Root of Jesse will spring up,
one who will arise to *rule over the nations;*
in him the Gentiles will hope." Romans 15:8–12

Verses 8–9 are a clear reference to promises of Genesis 12:3 where God vowed to bless Abraham and through his Seed to bless all nations! Paul reinforces this with a series of Old Testament passages where the nations would eventually make their way to Jesus! "All the Gentiles! All the people's! All Israel" praising God for His saving mercy which we have seen eventually becomes a reality!

So what has Paul told us? First of all, salvation, which includes eternal destiny, is in the hands of God. Salvation is by grace alone. God has planned the salvation of whole of humanity through His mystery. First the remnant of Israel is saved, this is followed by the full number of Gentiles coming in, this in turn triggers the unsaved Jews to salvation–envy which then leads them to enter into salvation when Jesus returns which will be followed by the salvation of all the nations that had rejected Jesus. So in this way Paul speaks in harmony with what we have read in the prophets. The eventual and ultimate restoration of Israel will trigger a pilgrimage of all nations to Jesus.

This idea is picked up in the book of Revelation where we read that all nations eventually enter into the New Jerusalem [whose dimensions are in proportion to the Temple!] through the gates to meet the church who is inside waiting for them.

Let's turn to Revelation now.

CHAPTER SEVEN

All The Nations And Kings Will Worship With The Saints

In the following two chapters I will demonstrate that all nations eventually make their pilgrimage to God at the very end of time after the final judgment, in fact after and through the lake of fire. This brings to fulfilment the promise made to Abraham—that God will bless all nations through Abraham's Seed.

I will focus on two primary passages in Revelation: the first is Revelation 15:2–4. These verses, when understood in context, I believe present one of the most powerful defences for Universalism in the whole Bible.

> [2] And I *saw* something like a sea of glass mixed with fire, and *those who had been victorious over the beast* and his image and the number of his name, standing on the sea of glass, *holding harps of God*. [3] And they sang the song of

Moses, the bond-servant of God, and the song of the Lamb, saying,

"Great and marvelous are Your works,
O Lord God, the Almighty;
Righteous and true are Your ways,
King of the nations!
[4] "Who will not fear, O Lord, and glorify your name?
For You alone are holy;

For all the nations will come and worship before you,
For Your righteous acts have been revealed."
(Revelation 15:2–4 NASB)

Who are these that are singing this song of victory? At what point in time are they singing this song? Who are the "all the nations" that will eventually come and worship God? And finally what does John mean when he says that "Your righteous acts have been revealed"?

These verses unambiguously refer to a point in time when **all the nations** make their pilgrimage to God and worship him in fulfilment of everything we have been studying so far.

Who are these that are singing this song of victory and at what time in history are they singing it? The text speaks for itself. Those singing this song of victory are the saved who have already gone through the final crisis described in Revelation 13–14. We are told specifically that this group with harps in their hands had already been victorious over the beast, his image and the number of his name. All of these events are described in Chapter 13. The means that the events of 15:2–4 are future to those in chapters 13–14!

In these earlier chapters we read of some point in history where the whole world follows after the beast, worships him and his image and eventually receives the number of his name. See Revelation 13:3–4,

14–18. This universal language makes it clear that nothing like this has ever happened in the history of mankind. It is clearly future. It speaks of a time when the whole world will worship this counterfeit trinity, given it will worship the dragon, the beast and the image of the beast! Those who believe that these events refer to the destruction of Jerusalem in 70 AD have not taken into account the worldwide scope of what is being described here. We have never reached a point in history yet that describes a worldwide worship that is forced! Clearly the end of time is in view.

This is further supported by the following chapter. In Chapter 14 we see how the church responds to this worldwide enforced, worship crisis. In response to this crisis the church calls the world to refuse to worship the beast, its image or receive the number of its name (Revelation 14:9–11). The following verse then describes a class of who remain faithful. Here they are identified.

> [12] Here is the perseverance of *the saints* who keep the commandments of God and *their faith in Jesus.*
> (Revelation 14:12)

We are left with no doubt here. We have two groups described: the nations who worship the beast and the saints who remain faithful to Jesus! Those who remain faithful are Christians; their faith rests solely in Jesus. With this information in hand we can now return to the text and draw some initial conclusions.

> [2] And I saw something like a sea of glass mixed with fire, and *those who had been victorious over the beast* and his image and the number of his name, standing on the sea of glass, holding harps of God. [3] And they sang the song of Moses, the bond-servant of God, and the song of the Lamb (Revelation 15:2 NASB)

Here we are presented with the church after the final crisis is over. The events of Chapters 13–14 are clearly in the past. Their faith in Jesus has remained intact. They are holding harps of God and sing. What does this mean? We have an identical passage earlier on in the book with many points of contact.

> [1] Then I looked, and behold, the Lamb *was* standing on Mount Zion, and with Him one hundred and forty-four thousand, having His name and the name of His Father written on their foreheads. [2] And I heard a voice from heaven, like the sound of many waters and like the sound of loud thunder, and the voice which I heard *was* like *the sound* of harpists playing on their harps.
>
> [3] And they sang a new song before the throne and before the four living creatures and the elders; and no one could learn the song except the one hundred and forty-four thousand who had been purchased from the earth.
>
> [4] These are the ones who have not been defiled with women, for they have kept themselves chaste. These *are* the ones who follow the Lamb wherever He goes. These have been purchased from among men as first fruits to God and to the Lamb. (Revelation 14:1–5 NASB)

The parallels are powerful and obvious. Both passages speak about a group of humans who remain faithful to the lamb, playing harps, singing songs to the Lamb and are *before the throne*!

It is clear that what we are reading in Revelation 15:2–4 is a description of the church *after the final crisis* before the throne in the presence of Jesus singing songs of praise to him.

Back in Chapter 14 we read of another significant event that immediately precedes this worship scene in heaven.

Immediately after the church proclaims its final warning to the nations of the earth we are told that some believers will die at this time as a result of their message. Note how verses 12–14 flow into one another.

> [12] Here is the perseverance of the saints who keep the commandments of God and their faith in Jesus.
>
> [13] And I heard a voice from heaven, saying, "Write, 'Blessed are the dead who die in the Lord from now on!'" "Yes," says the Spirit, "so that they may rest from their labors, for their deeds follow with them."
>
> [14] Then I looked, and behold, a white cloud, and sitting on the cloud *was* one like a son of man (Revelation 14:12–14 NASB)

It is clear. These chapters describe world events that culminate with the return of Jesus on the clouds of heaven. Following this we read that those who have remained faithful to Jesus at this time, including those who have died, find themselves before the throne after the final crisis singing a song that proclaims the message that the nations, those who actually persecuted them [I will show this later] will one day join in with them before the throne and worship. The pilgrimage of all nations will take place!

John refers to the church as the "first fruits" to God. This is important.

First Fruits: The Promise of a Universal Harvest

The idea of first fruits has a significant back story. In Old Testament times the Israelites would gather together their choicest and earliest ripened portion of their crops and would offer them to God in gratitude. It also functioned as a guarantee and foretaste of *the greater harvest to follow*. This is important to understand as we shall see. For now we need to keep one thing clearly in mind. This group has come out from the nations—they come out from them and are distinct from them now as followers of the Lamb (Rev 14:4)—more on this soon.

This idea as the church as the first fruits is reinforced in the New Testament. In Romans 16:5 Epenetus is called the "first fruits unto Christ" meaning that he was the first convert in that area which was the guarantee of a future and greater harvest of believers.

In 1 Corinthians 15:20 Jesus is called the "first fruits of them that have fallen asleep." Jesus was the pledge and guarantee of the greater harvest that will follow when the saved dead are raised back to life at the Second Coming of Jesus. Compare 1 Corinthians 15:23 with 1 Thessalonians 4:13–18.

In the exact same way, the saints, the 144,000 who go through the final crisis are presented as the first fruits to God. As first fruits they guarantee the eventual *final* crop. They are described as standing before the throne singing a song of victory and proclaim that the final harvest will follow them as the first fruit offering!

So given the church is already before the throne, given that the final crisis is already over, given that Jesus has already returned to the earth and given that they are functioning as the first fruits to God, then what final harvest could there be following all of this? Obviously as the first fruits they are not in themselves this final harvest! What is this greater harvest? Where does it come from? The text provides the answer!

As first fruits they are already before the throne worshiping God. And in songs of praise they speak of a greater harvest of worshippers: they proclaim in song that *all the nations will one day come and join them in worship.* The nations who persecuted them are the rest of the crop! Remember that they were those taken from the nations!

This is a big call to make so I will need to spend some time here to substantiate this vital point.

Whatever follows, the point is clear that *all nations will one day come and join them in worship*! Since the ones singing this song are those who have remained faithful to Jesus [the saved] then who else can the nations represent?

Does John definitively identify who the nations are in Revelation? Let's consider every time the word "nations" appears in Revelation and see if it refers consistently to some specific group.

Who Are the "Nations" in Revelation?

First of all we are told in the passage at hand that God is "King of the nations." Revelation 15:3. In the next verse we read that "ALL the nations will come and worship" the "King of the nations"! To fully see the Universalist implications of this we need to carefully identify who the "nations" are in verse 4.

I will now refer to every single instance in Revelation—through Chapter 20, up to the New Heavens and New Earth—where the word "nations" appears. Since there are so many references I would ask you to read all the verses that I refer to and notice how the word "nations" functions in these verses. You will see that in every single case the "nations" refers to the people groups of the world who reject God and persecute His people. This point is absolutely critical to understand. It is only after we understand this important point that Revelation 15:2–4 can be given its full contextual and radical universalistic force. So please take time to read every reference to "nations" that I am going to direct you to.

- Christ will grant his authority to the Saints to rule over the nations (2:26)

- The Saints praise the Lamb, who purchased them from every nation to be kings and priests (5:9)

- The multitude before the Lamb came out from every nation (7:9)

- John prophesies against the nations (10:11)

- People of the nations gaze upon the bodies of the witnesses and refuse them burial (11:9)

- The 24 Elders sing of the nations who were angry, and God's wrath is come (11:18)

- The Woman gave birth to the male son to rule the nations with an iron scepter (12:5)

- The Beast is given power over the nations, who worship the Beast, and make war against the saints with him (13:7)

- The Angel proclaims the eternal gospel to the nations, and announce the coming judgment (14:6)

- But the nations ignore the warning, and instead the nations drink the maddening wine of Babylon's adulteries, and so will share her fate, to drink the wine of the wrath of God, and be tormented in the presence of the Lamb (14:8-11)

- The victorious saints sing and prophesy that all nations will come and worship the Lord, who is King of the nations

- But as the bowls are poured, the cities of the nations collapse, and Babylon gets the cup of God's wrath (15:3-5)

- The angel tells John that the Prostitute sits on the waters, which are the nations (17:15)

- The angels laments the fall and corruption of Babylon, as the nations drank the wine of her adulteries (18:3)

- The angel proclaims Babylon's doom, as she has led all the nations astray by her magic spell (18:23)

- Christ appears on his horse, carrying a sharp sword to strike down the nations, as he will rule over the nations (19:15; cf Psalm 2:9)

- The devil is thrown into the Abyss, to keep him from deceiving the nations (20:3)

- As soon as he is released, he deceives the nations, who gather with him for battle (20:8)

- When the nations march upon God's people with Satan, they are devoured by fire; the Beast is thrown into the lake of fire, where they also go, along with all whose name is not found in the Book of Life (20:7-15)

The point is this: never once do we read that the saints are identified with the nations. They are on opposing sides. The nations are the people groups of the world that constitute the world in rebellion against God. This is unequivocally clear in Revelation!

The saints are in fact distinguished from the nations by John. The saints are those "redeemed out of the nations" (5:9; 7:9) to form a new kingdom and are the objects of Satan's rage through the nations (11:18; 12:17).

So there can be no doubt whatsoever that the nations in Revelation in 15:2–4 refers to same group as those nations that end up in the lake of fire! John has used this word consistently right throughout the book and there is never an exception to this rule. To try and insist that the "nations" refers to godly powers is to break with the consistent contextual usage of John throughout the book.

Additionally, in 15:2–4 the nations cannot be the saints! The saints, who are clearly the saved, are singing about a future time when another group called "the nations" will join in with them and worship the God who is *King of the nations*! The verses clearly distinguish the saints from the nations who are yet to follow! The saints are the first fruits harvest and have come from the nations and they guarantee a greater harvest yet to come—the nations from which they came!

So what does the victory song of the saints tell us about the destiny of the nations? We are told that although they are currently experiencing the wrath of God they still "will," future tense, come and worship God. This is after their time in this fire (14:9–11; 20:10–15). Remember that the nations who join forces with Satan at the end of the 1000 years appear before God in the final judgment and are cast into the lake of fire (20:7–15). We are told that whoever does not have their names written in the book of life end up in the lake of fire (20:11–15). The nations have been at war with God and His people right up till the time of the great white throne judgment scene. They end up in the lake of fire! If it is not them then who else is left? All we have is two groups: the saints and the nations and given the saints are in the book of life then the text is clear that it can only be the unrepentant nations that end up in the lake of fire!

But given they will eventually join the saints in worship before God and given they are in the lake of fire this means that their stay in this place or condition is not endless! Given the unrepentant nations end up in the lake of fire which burns "forever and ever" and given the nations will join the church in worship before the throne then this means that "forever and ever" does not and cannot mean endless.

Please note that John does not say that *some* people from all the nations will come and worship but that *all* nations will come and worship!

I will now demonstrate that although the nations had rejected God and the everlasting Gospel and even though they will find themselves in the lake of fire, they can still come to repentance and accept the Good News—and will do so, and so join in with the saints before the throne in worship.

Revelation 14:6–7 speaks of the final proclamation of the Gospel to the world: "I saw an angel preaching the everlasting Gospel to all nations." Verses 9–11 tell us that the nations reject the Gospel and so experience the wrath of God. As we have seen, the saints in 15:2–4 are described in heaven after the final crisis is over and sings of a future time when the rejecters of the Gospel will one day join in with them before the throne in worship.

What has been missed is this: the song that the saints sing tells the story that the nations during their stay in the lake of fire finally repent and accept the everlasting Gospel. Note the following precise points of contact between the song the saints sing and the content of the everlasting Gospel in Chapter 14!

I will address this by considering the following questions: is the future worship of the nations forced or willing? What does the song mean when the saints proclaim that the "the nations will come and worship because you have revealed your righteous acts (or righteousness)"? Are the righteous acts of God damnatory or restorative? Finally, what relationship is there between the song of the saints and the content of the everlasting Gospel of Revelation 14:6–7?

Forced or Willing Worship By the Nations

Is it possible that the nations forcibly worship God? Let's consider the immediate setting again and see if their worship is forced or willing. John clearly alludes to Psalm 86 in this passage. Note the similarities.

> [9] *All nations* whom You have made shall come
> and worship before You, O Lord,
> And they shall glorify Your name.
> [10] For You are great and do wondrous deeds;
> You alone are God. (Psalm 86:9–10 NASB)

And,

> [3] And they sang the song of Moses, the bond-servant of God,
> and the song of the Lamb, saying,
>
> "Great and marvelous are Your works,
> O Lord God, the Almighty;
> Righteous and true are Your ways,
> King of the nations!
> [4] "Who will not fear, O Lord, and glorify Your name?
> For You alone are holy;
> *For all the nations will come and worship before You,*
> *For Your righteous acts have been revealed.*" (Revelation 15:3–4 NASB)

Both passages refer to "all nations," "great and marvellous deeds," "glorifying God," "you alone" and "all nations" coming to "worship." The points of contact are obvious and too many to ignore. There is nothing in Psalms 86 that suggests forced worship; and neither is there in Revelation 15! Given the obvious reference to Psalm 86 it is clear that the universal worship is volunteered and a loving response! The fact is that later we read that the nations find healing as they enter into the New Jerusalem (22:1–5).

The Restorative Righteous Acts of God

John raises the question "who will not fear and glorify" you? The answer follows the question: "No one will, for all the nations will come and worship before you!" Why? Because: "Your righteous acts have been revealed!" The point is this: the "righteous acts" or righteousness of God in the Old Testament results in acts of rescue, deliverance and salvation (Daniel 9:16; Psalm 71:2, 15-19). See also 1 Samuel 12:7; Judges 5:11; Psalm 98:2; 143:11 ; Isaiah 46:13; 51:5–8; 56:1; 59:16; 61:10; Micah 6:4-5; Zechariah 8:8. When God manifests His righteousness, salvation results and it is for this reason that John is telling us that all nations at some time in the future will come and worship God as restored saints!

The Eternal Gospel and the Nations

But there is stronger contextual evidence that demonstrates that the nations can and do repent and so accept the everlasting gospel even during their stay in the lake of fire. The saints raise two questions in this song and answer them in connection with the everlasting Gospel. They raise two questions: Who will not fear God *and* who will not glorify him? What many have missed is the direct contextual link back to Revelation 14:6–7. Let's compare these passages.

> [6] And I saw another angel flying in midheaven, having an ***eternal gospel to preach to*** those who live on the earth, and to every **nation** and tribe and tongue and people; [7] and he said with a loud voice, ***"fear God***, and give Him ***glory,*** because the hour of His judgment has come; ***worship Him*** who made the heaven and the earth and sea and springs of waters." Revelation (14:6–7 NASB)

Now put this together with the passage at hand.

> [3] And they sang the song of Moses, the bond-servant of God, and the song of the Lamb, saying,

"Great and marvelous are Your works,
O Lord God, the Almighty;
Righteous and true are Your ways,
King of the nations!

⁴ "Who will not FEAR, O Lord, and GLORIFY Your name?
For You alone are holy;
For *all the nations will come and worship You*,
For Your righteous acts have been revealed."
(Revelation 15:3–4 NASB)

The parallels are stunningly obvious, and should not be ignored. We read in 14:6–7 that this eternal Gospel goes out to the "*nations*." He also tells us that the only appropriate response of *faith* to the eternal Gospel is to **fear God, glorify God and as a result worship God**! The response of those who accept the everlasting Gospel then is that they: "fear God, give glory to him and worship him"!

Then we read in Chapter 15 that the nations at some time in the future will do exactly that: **fear God, glorify him and worship him**! John says that none of the nations will not fear God, none will not glorify him, for all will come and worship God! The nations can and will accept the everlasting Gospel. Here is proof positive for post-death and even post judgment evangelism, repentance and salvation!

John has used his terms very carefully and draws unmistakable parallels. He tells us in the clearest contextual terms possible that some time after the crisis is over, after the nations have ended up in the lake of fire that the nations will end up accepting the King of the Nations: they fear God, give him glory and end up in worship alongside the saints they persecuted and martyred!

He even goes onto tell us that to glorify God means the same thing as repent!

⁹ Men were scorched with fierce heat; and they blasphemed the name of God who has the power over these plagues, and they did not *repent so as to give Him glory*.
(Revelation 16:9 NASB)

Yes, even during the seven last plagues God is calling the nations to repent! To repent means the same thing as to glorify God. Given that the nations will eventually glorify God this means they hear the Gospel, repent and turn to faith in Jesus sometime after they have experienced the wrath of God in 14:9–11!

So when in history does this event actually take place?

We are not left in the dark on this important issue. The closing chapters of Revelation record the fulfilment of this promise! Here we will read that the nations exit the lake of fire and enter into the Temple to worship God! As they enter through the city gates they eat from the leaves of the tree of life connected to the throne and find their final healing.

Can this be true? Read on.

CHAPTER EIGHT

"Behold I Am *Making* All Things New" Revelation 21

So do the nations make their pilgrimage to the Temple and meet with God and worship him? But how can they? So far we have them in the lake of fire! Can they exit? Do they exit? What must they do to exit? Are there any conditions?

We have seen that Revelation 15:2–4 promised they would and it is now in the latter chapters of Revelation that we read that it actually happens.

What John does in these final chapters is bring in all the themes we have been looking at so far in the Bible. He speaks about justice, wrath, judgment, the Garden of Eden—God declares war on sin and finally eradicates it and by so doing restores His children in the process.

So, we have arrived at the end.

The judgment is over. The New Jerusalem descends from heaven on earth made new. But wait! We find something strange. The nations are entering into the city through its gates.

> ²⁴ The **nations** will **walk by its light**, and the kings of the earth will bring their splendor **into it**. ²⁵ On no day will its gates ever be shut, for there will be no night there. ²⁶ The glory and honor of **the nations** will be brought into it. ²⁷ Nothing impure will ever enter it, nor will anyone who does what is shameful or deceitful, but only those **whose names are written in the Lamb's book of life.** (Revelation 21:24–27)

What is happening here? We have already seen that the nations were enemies of God and of His people in every single passage in this book and now they enter into the city to meet up with the saints.

And there is a paradox.

> ¹⁴ "Blessed are those who wash their robes, that they may have the right to the tree of life and may go through the gates into the city. (Revelation 22:14)

On the one hand it is only those whose names are written in the Lamb's book of life that can enter into the city and on the other hand the nations, the enemies of God enter into it! And further, a person can only have their names recorded in the book of life by washing their robes in the blood of the Lamb! What has happened?

The nations have had their names recorded in the Lamb's book by washing their robes in the blood of the Lamb! John says that no one can ever enter into the city in an impure state. The nations have finally met the condition of entry and this after the final judgment and after the lake of fire! They have finally washed their robes in the blood of the lamb—they are no longer impure! Praise God!

But more:

> [1] Then the angel showed me the river of the water of life, as
> clear as crystal, flowing from the throne of God and of the
> Lamb [2] down the middle of the great street of the city. On
> each side of the river stood **the tree of life**, bearing twelve
> crops of fruit, yielding its fruit every month. And **the leaves
> of the tree are for the healing of the nations.**
> (Revelation 22:1–3)

Eden has been restored! The tree and river of life reappear and the
nations who have entered into the city through its gates eat from its
leaves and are healed! What?! Yes! We are now clearly in the eternal
blessed state and we read of nations requiring healing?! We have
come full circle. The covenant with Abraham to restore the nations
back to Edenic origins has been fulfilled.

The nations surrender to Jesus by washing their robes in the blood of
the Lamb, their names are recorded in the Lamb's book of life, they
enter into the city and inside the city, right in front of the throne of
God and of the Lamb, and they eat from Eden's leaves and find their
healing. Peace.

Question: how did the nations get from rejecting Jesus to finally
entering into the New Jerusalem, and this after the judgment and lake
of fire?

Didn't the nations end up in the lake of fire? Then how is it that they
are now entering into the city to meet up with the saints in Eden
restored?

We need to camp here a little and do some further narrative analysis
and connect the dots. Let's take a step back and fill in the unfolding
story described in Chapters 19–22.

Before the final restoration John speaks of war and theodicy in chapters 19–20. God acts in warfare against sin to eradicate it once and for all! In doing so He returns to the violent metaphors we found in the Old Testament. But one thing is certain: just like the Old Testament we find that universal restoration is clearly in view. God takes action to eradicate sin once and for all and in the process restore His children and His fallen creation. God will not abandon His fallen creation; He will work with it and restore it.

This idea is brought out in the following verse.

> [5] He who was seated on the throne said, "*I am making everything* new!" Then he said, "Write this down, for these words are trustworthy and true." (Revelation 21:5)

And the words that just came before them?

> Then I saw "a new heaven and a new earth," for the first heaven and the first earth had passed away,
> (Revelation 21:1)

So we are clearly in the eternal, perfect state. Can you see the puzzle? In verse one we are told that God has *already* made a new heaven and earth. This begs the question: since a new heaven and earth have already been made, what else is there to make new after this in verse five? Doesn't a new heaven and earth constitute everything that can exist?

Did you notice that John uses the present continuous tense? "*I am making*." This "making new" is a process that continues on in the era of the new heaven and earth. So what exactly is God going to make new in an already completed new heaven and new earth? What is left that needs to be made new?

We are even told that God is going to make *"everything"* new. But doesn't the "new heaven and earth" that has already been made include "everything"? Obviously not! So what remains that needs to be made new? John targets those in the lake of fire—they are part of this "everything" that will be made new. Let's see how this happens.

As we read Revelation 21 through it becomes obvious that the human race is still divided into two classes: we have those inside the city and those outside the city and in fact in the lake of fire. The bride, also called the saints (19:7–8), is identified with the New Jerusalem and is inside of it (21:2–9). They are contrasted with those who are in the lake of fire which is just outside the gates of the city! I will demonstrate this shortly.

The beginning of Revelation 21 talks about a new heaven, a new earth and the New Jerusalem descending down from heaven.

> [1] Then I saw "a new heaven and a new earth," for the first heaven and the first earth had passed away, and there was no longer any sea. [2] I saw the Holy City, the new Jerusalem, coming down out of heaven from God, prepared as a bride beautifully dressed for her husband. (Revelation 21:1–2)

We are clearly in the eternal blessed state. The church has descended onto the earth made new.

Then we find the description of those in the lake of fire at this same time

> [8] But the cowardly, the unbelieving, the vile, the murderers, the sexually immoral, those who practice magic arts, the idolaters and all liars—they will be consigned to the fiery lake of burning sulfur. This is the second death."
> (Revelation 21:8)

The "but" is used by John to contrast those in the lake of fire with those inside the New Jerusalem: "I saw the New Jerusalem, the bride... *But,* the … are consigned to the lake of fire." John will talk about two groups in the blessed eternal state: one group is inside the gates of the city and the other outside the gates and in the lake of fire. Let me now demonstrate this.

He starts off by mentioning both groups in verses 1–8 and then he focuses on the New Jerusalem in greater detail in verses 9–21.

We read that the bride is inside the city and what is significant is that the nations in the lake of fire are just outside its gates! And it is here that we are startled. We read that the nations inside the lake of fire actually start a procession, a pilgrimage, as they enter into the New Jerusalem and in through its gates. The prophecies of the Old Testament are finding their ultimate fulfilment!

Let's consider the footsteps of the nations in these latter chapters. Jesus, the Word of God, is presented as returning to earth for the final battle.

> [11] I saw heaven standing open and there before me was a white horse, whose rider is called Faithful and True. With justice he judges and wages war. [12] His eyes are like blazing fire, and on his head are many crowns. He has a name written on him that no one knows but he himself. [13] He is dressed in a robe dipped in blood, and his name is the Word of God. (Revelation 19:11–13)

Please remember that John has made it clear right in the first verse of the book that this book is in sign language and not to be taken literally.

The fact is this: there were many books around in the first century that read like John's book! It was a common genre of literature filled with bizarre images. But John's book is different! He uses similar images and then subverts them! The lion of Judah defeats the enemy by becoming a slain Lamb! So don't get side tracked by the language. It was common for the day and John really subverts a lot of it.

Anyway, as Jesus approaches the earth, the nations turn on him but are defeated.

> [14] The armies of heaven were following him, riding on white horses and dressed in fine linen, white and clean. [15] Coming out of his mouth is a sharp sword with which to strike down *the nations*. (Revelation 19:14–15)

Satan is then described as being bound for 1000 years—he cannot deceive the nations during this period in 20:3 so as "to keep him from deceiving the *nations* anymore until the thousand years were ended. After that, he must be set free for a short time."

After the 1000 year period we read that the nations are still opposed to Jesus and his people.

> [7] When the thousand years are over, Satan will be released from his prison [8] and will go out to deceive *the nations* in the four corners of the earth—Gog and Magog—and *to gather them for battle*. In number they are like the sand on the seashore. [9] They marched across the breadth of the earth and surrounded the camp of God's people, the city He loves. But fire came down from heaven and devoured them. (Revelation 20:7–9)

It is obvious that the nations are still opposed to Jesus at this point.

It is now that we read of the Great White Throne Judgment scene.

The nations have rejected Jesus up till this point right throughout the book of Revelation. Now they are judged.

[11] Then I saw a great white throne and him who was seated on it. The earth and the heavens fled from his presence, and there was no place for them. [12] And I saw the dead, great and small, standing before the throne, and books were opened. Another book was opened, which is the book of life. The dead were judged according to what they had done as recorded in the books.

[15] Anyone whose name was not found written in the book of life was thrown into the lake of fire. (Revelation 20:11–15)

The nations have made war with Jesus, were struck down by the sword coming out of his mouth (clearly a symbol!), and were devoured after the 1000 year period—they have not submitted to King Jesus. They now stand in judgment to reveal this very thing. Their names are clearly not found in the Lamb's book of life. They have not washed their robes in the blood of the Lamb and now are consigned to the lake of fire.

They are then mentioned again in Chapter 21 in the eternal blessed state as we have already noticed.

[8] But the cowardly, the unbelieving, the vile, the murderers, the sexually immoral, those who practice magic arts, the idolaters and all liars—they will be consigned to the fiery lake of burning sulfur. This is the second death." (Revelation 21:8)

But now things change.

We read that the nations walk into the city and through its gates.

[24] The *nations* will walk by its light, and the kings of the earth will bring their splendor *into it*. [25] On *no day will its gates ever be shut*, for there will be no night there. [26] The

> glory and honor of the ***nations will be brought into it.*** *²⁷*
> ***Nothing impure will ever enter it,*** nor will anyone who does
> what is shameful or deceitful, but ***only those whose names***
> ***are written*** in the Lamb's book of life. (Revelation 21:24–
> 27)

We are told here that the nations enter into the city through its gates
which are always left open for them. Whilst they remain impure they
will never enter into the city. They must have their names written in
the Lamb's book of life and given the nations are in fact entering into
the city it is clear that they have indeed surrendered to Jesus. As they
surrender to Jesus they leave the lake of fire.

Revelation 22 mentions them again.

> ¹⁴ "Blessed are ***those who wash their robes***, that they may
> have the right to the tree of life and may ***go through the***
> ***gates into the city.*** ¹⁵ ***Outside*** [the gates] ***are*** [not will be!]
> the dogs, those who practice magic arts, the sexually
> immoral, the murderers, the idolaters and everyone who
> loves and practices falsehood. (Revelation 22:14–15)

Notice that here again we read of two groups: those who wash their
robes in the blood of the Lamb and so enter into the city through its
gates. But then we see a radical contrast: "those outside" the gates
cannot enter. The descriptive list provided is similar to the ones we
have already read. And now we find that the lake of fire is just
"outside" the gates.

And the Good News is that these gates are never shut for them! The
lake of fire is placed right next to the New Jerusalem and right outside
its gates! Only those who wash their robes may enter into the gates
and gain access to the tree of life!

But wait a minute. Earlier on in this same chapter we are told that the tree of life has been placed in the Garden for the nations and only appears after God and His throne have descended to the earth made new.

> Then the angel showed me *the river of the water of life*, as clear as crystal, flowing from the throne of God and of the Lamb ² down the middle of the great street of the city. On each side of the river stood the tree of life, bearing twelve crops of fruit, yielding its fruit every month. And *the leaves of the tree are for the healing of the nations.* (Revelation 22:1–2)

Wow! There is a lot in these verses! First of all we can be sure that that 22:14–15 is set at the time the eternal blessed state. How can we be so sure? For one thing we are told that the tree of life appears in front of the throne of God and the Lamb which only takes place after they have descended from heaven to earth made new. The tree of life is about the new earth and the Garden of Eden. And 22:14–15 has people outside the gates who need to enter into the city through the gates and eat from the leaves of the tree of life and so be healed!

To reinforce this interpretation we even read the following:

> ¹⁴ "Blessed are *those who wash* their robes, that they may *have the right to the tree of life* and may *go through the gates into the city.* ¹⁵ Outside are* the dogs, those who practice magic arts, the sexually immoral, the murderers, the idolaters and everyone who loves and practices falsehood. (Revelation 22:14–15)

Did you notice that these verses says "outside ARE"—not will be! John is talking about a time where there are two groups: those who are inside the city and those who "are" not are outside its gates.

But wait: an invitation is made to those outside the gates and in the lake of fire!

> [17] *The Spirit and the bride say, "Come!"* And let the one who hears say, "Come!" *Let the one who is thirsty come;* and let the one who wishes *take the free gift of the water of life.* (Revelation 22:17)

Wow again! Have you ever read these verses together before like this? Remember that when we read of the tree of life or the water of life or even about the "bride" we know we are reading of events taking place in the eternal blessed state on the earth made new. The Bride of Jesus, which appears in the book of Revelation only after the holy city and throne of God descends onto the new earth, makes an invitation to a group who are "thirsty": come and drink from the water of life which flows from the river of life which finds its origins at the throne of God. This is post mortem evangelism pure and simple!

> [22] Then the angel showed me *the river of the water of life*, as clear as crystal, flowing from the throne of God and of the Lamb (Revelation 22:1)

But before they can do this they must first wash in the blood of the Lamb to gain entry into the city through its gates!

And it is now, at this time, that those inside the lake of fire just outside the gates of the city are beckoned to "come"; to wash their robes so that they have can have their spiritual thirst quenched by drinking of the free gift of the water of life flowing from the river of life which comes straight from the throne of God and of the Lamb (Revelation 22:1–5).

They repent. They give glory to God and worship him as predicted in 15:2–4. They have accepted the everlasting Gospel as we have seen in the previous chapter. As they surrender to Jesus they are no longer impure for they have washed their robes in the blood of the Lamb and have had their names recorded in the book of life.

Fire in Revelation and the "Lake of Fire"

First of all, the Greek word translated "fire" is *pur*—we have borrowed this word in English to form the words "pure, purify, purification, purge." This word is about cleansing and purification. We have been told that those in the lake are "impure" and cannot enter into the city through its gates until they **wash**! Can you see this? They are impure and need to wash so that they can enter through the gates and into the city to meet up with the bride who is already inside waiting for them and calling them to wash in the blood of the lamb and get clean! Those in the lake of fire [purification] have been consigned there by God for a wash in the blood of the Lamb. That's what the lake is about.

This is why the lake of fire is right there just outside the gates of the city. They can hear and see folks inside preaching the Gospel to them: "wash in the blood and have your name recorded in the book of life and enter inside here with us"! Wow!

Secondly, fire in the book of Revelation is closely associated with the refining presence of God.

In 1:14 we read that the eyes of Jesus were like "blazing fire." This same description is found in 19:12.

In 3:18 we are told that "fire" *from Jesus* refines!

> I counsel you to buy *from me* gold *refined in the fire*, so you can become rich; and *white clothes* to wear, so you can

> ***cover your shameful nakedness***; and salve to put on your eyes, so you can see. (Revelation 3:18)

Fire is connected with being refined ("from me"!!) and with clean white clothes that cover nakedness and result in spiritual eyesight! This is significant!

In 8:5 "fire" is connected with the seven trumpets.

> Then the angel took the censer, filled it with ***fire from the altar***, and hurled it on the earth; and there came peals of thunder, rumblings, flashes of lightning and an earthquake. Then the seven angels who had the seven trumpets prepared to sound them. (Revelation 8:5–6)

In 8:5 "fire" comes "from the altar" of God and releases seven trumpet–plagues which are solely intended to bring about repentance and salvation.

> [20] The rest of mankind ... ***still did not repent*** of the work of their hands; they did not stop worshiping demons, and idols of gold, silver, bronze, stone and wood—***idols*** that cannot see or hear or walk. [21] Nor did they repent of their ***murders***, their ***magic arts, their sexual immorality*** or their thefts. (Revelation 9:20–21)

Did you notice how this group is described in similar terms to those in the lake of fire? Revelation 22:15: " ***Outside*** [the gates] ***are*** [not will be!] the dogs, those who practice ***magic arts, the sexually immoral***, the murderers, the ***idolaters*** and everyone who loves and practices falsehood."

Both speak about: "magic arts, sexual immorality, murders, idolatry." The former and the latter both experience fire! And it is clear in the former that the fire they experience is intended to produce repentance unto salvation!

John goes out of his way to say that the "rest of mankind STILL did not repent!" The whole way through the seven trumpet plagues God was only trying to bring unbelievers to repentance and salvation. The same is true in the seven plagues which also include fire!

> [8] The *fourth angel poured out his bowl on the sun*, and the sun was allowed to scorch people with *fire*. [9] They were seared by the intense heat and *they cursed the name of God, who had control over these plagues, but they refused to repent and glorify him.* (Revelation 16:8–9)

Can you see what is happening here? We are seeing a consistent picture emerge: the purpose of fire is to bring about repentance and salvation. Fire intends to cleanse and refine!

But back to the seven trumpets.

We have read that mankind, the nations, have refused to come to repentance and salvation through these plagues. Until the sixth one that is!

The sixth trumpet begins—also called the second woe—starts in 9:13 and ends in 11:14. Prior to these verses we read of the fifth trumpet and after them we read of the seventh!

But something significant finally happens at the end of the sixth trumpet.

> [13] At that very hour there was a severe earthquake and *a tenth of the city collapsed*. Seven thousand people were killed in the earthquake, and the rest *feared God and gave glory to the God of heaven*.

> [14] The second woe has passed; the third woe is coming soon.
> (Revelation 11:13–14)

So a tenth of the city (later called Babylon) falls but the "rest" of Babylon "fears God and gives glory to him"! This phrase is significant in Revelation. It represents the content of the Gospel that saves! We already noticed this in the last chapter. And here it is again. Notice the parallels.

> [6] Then I saw another angel flying in midair, and he had the eternal gospel to proclaim to those who live on the earth—to every NATION [note he mentions the NATIONS in this context!], tribe, language and people. [7] He said in a loud voice, "**Fear God** and **give him glory**, because the hour of His judgment has come. **Worship him)**"
> (Revelation 14:6–7)

Back in the sixth trumpet we read that 90% of mankind, the nations, "fear God and give glory to him!" Only 10% falls! The two witnesses who proclaimed the Gospel in Chapter 11 have finally succeeded! Fire has come from their mouths and devoured the unbelief of 90% of the nations. See 11:3, 5. Only 10% of Babylon falls at this point. The rest accept the everlasting Gospel: they fear God and give him glory which 16:9 clearly says they repent!

Fire is clearly connected to refining, cleansing, repentance, salvation and worship in Revelation. We need to rid ourselves of our Western assumptions of what fire means!

When fire comes from God or His angels in Revelation the only intended result is salvation! And so we read in 20:15 that after the final judgment the rebellious nations are consigned to the lake of fire. From that place, they finally begin their pilgrimage to leave it and enter into the city through its gates since they eventually heed the invitation to wash away their impurities in the blood of the lamb!

I personally believe that the lake of fire and the blood of the lamb are the same thing! The fire and the blood both cleanse! God's people are cleansed with fire from God who is a consuming fire! (Hebrews 12:29).

Fire as a symbol is used right throughout the Bible for the cleansing presence of God. For example the burning bush was the holy presence of God. Moses was told to take of his "dirty, impure" sandals as he entered into the cleansing presence of God! God sent "fire" to Isaiah in Chapter 6 to cleanse him.

> [2] But who can endure the day of His coming? Who can stand when He appears? For He *will be like a refiner's fire* or a *launderer's soap*. [3] He will sit as a refiner and purifier of silver; He *will purify* (Malachi 3:2–3)

When God turns up as fire for His people—His fire acts as soap to wash, purify and refine!

The same thing applies to the nations in the Old Testament.

> [8] Therefore wait for me,"
> declares the LORD,
> "for the day I will stand up to testify.
> I have decided to assemble **the nations**,
> to gather the kingdoms
> and to **pour out My wrath** on them—
> all My fierce anger.
> **The whole world will be consumed
> by the fire** of My jealous anger.

⁹ "**Then I will purify the lips of the peoples,**
   that **all of them may call on the name of the LORD**
   and **serve him** shoulder to shoulder. (Zephaniah 3:8–9)

How clear is this? God says that a day is coming when He will gather together all "nations" for the final judgment! He will pour out His entire wrath as fire! The nations get "consumed" through this fire! We would think that this was the end for them but the next verse tells us that they end up "purified" in the words they speak so that they call on the name of the Lord and serve Him in unity!

Fire from God only cleanses and saves. This passage speaks about the same judgment found in Revelation 20! It is the final judgment of all mankind and we read that the fire saves! Fire saves! Remember that to save means to restore! This applies both for the people of God and the lost nations!

The New King James Version is even more to the point:

⁹ "For then I will *restore to the peoples* a pure language,
   That they all may call on the name of the LORD,
   To serve Him with one accord. (Zephaniah 3:9 NKJV)

God's fire at the last judgment only restores. It has consumed them all but they are all very much alive! To consume clearly is a figure of speech given they are still alive. What got consumed was their idolatrous words! Instead of calling on their gods in this chapter they will call on the Lord and are saved!

Jesus spoke about this same judgment. In the sheep and the goats we are told that the nations (goats) are gathered together and then cast into "eternal fire" and "punishment." Remember that fire means to purify in the Greek! And more to the point Jesus uses the Greek word "kolasis" which eminent Greek scholar, Prof. William Barclay[18], says only ever means to "prune" so as to produce fruit! The goats go into pruning, refining fire and the nations in the lake of fire wash their robes in the blood of the blood! Same thing!

What a marvellous consistent picture emerges!

Paul also uses fire as an image of cleansing.

> [13] Each man's work will become evident; for the Day will show it because it is *to be* **revealed with fire**, and **the fire itself will test** the quality of each man's work. [14] If any man's work which he has built on it remains, he will receive a reward. [15] If any **man's work is burned up**, he will suffer loss; but he **himself will be saved, yet so as through fire**. (1 Corinthians 3:13–15 NASB)

Paul speaks of the final judgment. He says that our "works" will be tested and revealed on that day. In context Paul is talking about believers who build their kingdom work on Jesus and those who don't! Those who were about building for their own glory—their works will be burned up on that day but they themselves will be saved (remember the Greek word sozo means to make whole and restore!) yet only as through fire (Greek to purify).

Fire removes refuse and bad works but leaves the person restored! This is exactly what we read in Zephaniah and is also the case in Revelation when the nations are consigned to the lake of purification, heed the call to wash in the blood of the lamb, are cleansed and then enter into the city through the gates, to drink from the water of the river of life, and eat from the leaves of the tree of life, both of which

---

[18] *William Barclay: A Spiritual Autobiography*, pg 65-67, William B Eerdmans Publishing Company, Grand Rapids, 1977. You can read his words at: http://www.auburn.edu/~allenkc/barclay1.html

flow from the healing throne of God! And so the story of the Bible ends.

> [1] Then the angel showed me the river of the water of life, as clear as crystal, flowing from the throne of God and of the Lamb [2] down the middle of the great street of the city. On each side of the river stood the tree of life, bearing twelve crops of fruit, yielding its fruit every month. And the leaves of the tree are for the healing of the nations. [3] No longer will there be any curse. The throne of God and of the Lamb will be in the city, and his servants will serve him. [4] They will see his face, and his name will be on their foreheads. [5] There will be no more night. They will not need the light of a lamp or the light of the sun, for the Lord God will give them light. And they will reign for ever and ever. (Revelation 22:1–5)

The nations wash themselves in the blood of the Lamb. They enter into the city through its gates and find their healing from the leaves of the tree of life which is right there at the throne of God. There will be no more curse.

Eden created, Eden fallen and now Eden restored. God's love affair with the nations comes to consummation. The promise of Genesis that Adam and Eve should fill the earth with inhabitants—later called the nations as we saw has come to fulfilment.

The promise to Abraham finally reaches an experiential reality!

> [18] In your seed all the nations of the earth shall be blessed (Genesis 22:18)

Paul tells us that the Seed is Jesus (Galatians 3:16). He also says that the blessing of the nations takes place as all accept the Gospel and so are saved and restored.

⁸ Scripture foresaw that **God would justify the Gentiles by faith**, and announced **the gospel** in advance to Abraham: "**All nations** will be blessed through you." (Galatians 3:8)

The blessing is the Gospel—the justification [putting back into proper working order] of all the nations!

And all means all for Paul as we have seen! Through the one act of righteousness of Jesus, all humanity is justified and has life (Romans 5:18). This objective truth finally works its way through human experience. All saved!

The nations finally make their pilgrimage to God. They come to Jesus. Eden is restored but with one difference. Adam never had the very throne and presence of God and Jesus with him! But at the end Father Son and Spirit all dwell with the nations on the earth restored and renewed. And they all lived happily ever after. Amen.

Appendix

Wait! What about the damnation texts?

> [10] They [the lost nations] will drink the wine of God's fury, which has been poured full strength into **the cup of His wrath**. They will be **tormented with burning sulphur** in the presence of the holy angels and of the Lamb. [11] And the **smoke of their torment will rise for ever and ever**. There will be **no rest day or night** for those who worship the beast and its image, or for anyone who receives the mark of its name." (Revelation 14:10–11)

In the previous chapters we saw that the nations who enter the lake of fire eventually exit it and enter into the New Jerusalem.

So how can we reconcile such statements that suggest permanent irreversible states of damnation, with the idea that the nations pass through them and into the New Jerusalem?

Revelation's Use of Old Testament Judgment Vocabulary

In the following sections, I will demonstrate now that all the above phrases are part and parcel of the judgment vocabulary and rhetoric of Old Testament prophets and are intended to trigger repentance and salvation and never suggest that the door of mercy is closed! And this is exactly what John is saying too, given the nations enter the New Jerusalem.

- The Cup of Wrath
- Sulphur, Smoke and Fire Forever
- Judgments, Plagues and Brimstone
- Final Judgment and Salvation
- My Thoughts on Retributive Justice

We'll explore whether this language necessarily excludes future salvation. Here we will consider how these statements are references to statements made—vocabulary used—by the Old Testament prophets, and how were they originally employed.

We will consider how judgment statements function in the book of Revelation, and whether they are permanently damnatory, or corrective. And finally, we'll consider how retributive judgments have a restorative end.

The Cup of God's Wrath

Let's start with the imagery of the "cup of God's wrath." Does this signify a permanent state of damnation?

This phrase is very common in the Old Testament. [19]

Consider Jeremiah.

> [15] This is what the LORD, the God of Israel, said to me: "Take from my hand this *cup filled with the wine of my wrath and*

---

[19] See Job 21:20; Psalm 60:3; 75:8; Jeremiah 49:12; Ezekiel 23:32-34; Obadiah 16

make all the nations to whom I send you *drink it.*[16] When they drink it, they will stagger and go mad because of the sword I will send among them."

[17] So I took the cup from the LORD's hand and made all the nations to whom He sent me drink it: [18] *Jerusalem* and the towns of Judah, its kings and officials, to make them a ruin and an object of horror and scorn, a curse—as they are today; [19] Pharaoh king of *Egypt*, his attendants, his officials and all his people (Jeremiah 25:15–19)

All nations including Israel can drink the very same wine from the same cup of God's wrath. There are not two different cups of wrath. Some have suggested that the cup of wrath for Israel means correction but for the nations it means damnation. This is not acceptable given this passage clearly paints a picture of all nations, including Israel drinking from the one cup. What happens to Israel when she drinks from the cup of wrath holds true for the nations.

But the point is this: drinking from the cup of wrath never describes a permanent irreversible state of damnation.

When John speaks of the "cup of wrath" he quotes Isaiah 51. Notice the similarities.

[17] *You* who have drunk from the hand of the LORD *the cup of His wrath*, you who have *drained to its dregs* (Isaiah 51:17)

Here the cup of God's wrath has been experienced to the full; down to its very dregs! How did they experience this "cup of wrath"?

[19] These double calamities have come upon you—who can comfort you?—ruin and destruction, famine and sword (Isaiah 51:19)

At this time Israel had been captive to Babylon! They were experiencing the curses of the broken covenant of Leviticus 26.

They had experienced God's cup of wrath to the full—right down to the very dregs—but was this a permanent irreversible state?

> [20] *They are filled with the wrath of the LORD,*
> with the rebuke of your God.

> [21] Therefore hear this ...
> [22] This is what your Sovereign LORD says,
> your God, *who defends his people*:

>> "See, *I have taken out of your hand*
>> *the cup* that made you stagger;
>> from that cup, *the goblet of my wrath*,
>> you will never drink again.

> [23] I will put it into the hands of your tormentors [Babylon],
> who said to you, 'Fall prostrate that we may walk on you.'
> And you made your back like the ground,
> like a street to be walked on." (Isaiah 51:20–23)

Can you see what is happening here? A person can experience the full cup of the wrath of God right down to its very dregs and yet this is not the end! God ends this experience and responds to this by "defending" them and finally removing and ending the cup of His wrath!

There is nothing inherent in this phrase to indicate a permanent state of damnation. To the contrary, salvation follows the full cup of God's wrath! One can drink of the cup of God's wrath and still pass from this to restoration! There is nothing present in this idea to mean that future hope of salvation is gone forever.

Sulphur, Smoke and Fire Forever

What about the smoke that ascends forever and the eternal fire mentioned in Revelation 14? Don't these suggest a permanent irreversible state of damnation?

John echoes the language of Sodom's destruction.

> **24** Then the LORD rained down *burning sulphur* on Sodom and Gomorrah—from the LORD out of the heavens. **25** Thus He overthrew those cities and the entire plain, *destroying all those living* in the cities—and also the vegetation in the land. **26** But Lot's wife looked back, and she became a pillar of salt.
>
> **27** Early the next morning Abraham got up and returned to the place where he had stood before the LORD. **28** He looked down toward Sodom and Gomorrah, toward all the land of the plain, and *he saw dense smoke rising from the land, like smoke from a furnace.* (Genesis 19:24–28)

Notice the parallels with Revelation 14: both speak about "fire," "burning sulphur" and even "rising smoke."

Jude describes Sodom as follows:

> **7** Likewise, Sodom and Gomorrah … serve as an example by undergoing a **punishment of eternal fire.** (Jude 1:7 NRSV)

Sodom experiences "eternal" fire and serves as a model for God's end-time judgment as explicitly outlined in Revelation. The fate of the lost world will be the same as that of Sodom!

The point is this: even such severe punishment results in restoration!

⁴⁹ This was the guilt of your sister Sodom and her daughters:
⁵⁰ They were haughty, and did abominable things before me;
therefore I removed them when I saw it. ⁵¹ Samaria has not
committed half your sins; you have committed more
abominations than they, and have made your sisters appear
righteous by all the abominations that you have committed.

⁵² Bear your disgrace, you also, for you have brought about
for your sisters a more favorable judgment; because of your
sins in which you acted more abominably than they, they are
more in the right than you. So be ashamed, you also, and
bear your disgrace, for you have made your sisters appear
righteous.

⁵³ *I will restore* their fortunes, the fortunes of **Sodom** and her
daughters and the fortunes of Samaria and her daughters, and
I will restore your own fortunes along with theirs (Ezekiel
16:50–53 NRSV)

Sodom experienced all the same features as the hell text in Revelation
14 and yet eventually will be restored! There is nothing in any of this
judgment rhetoric to suggest that people can't be saved even after the
most severe judgments! You have to bring these ideas and read them
into the text. Our Western conditioning has trained us to think in these
ways but Bible writers surely did not!

Did you notice that Abraham looked back onto Sodom and saw rising
smoke? The same thing is said of the lost nations: "the smoke of their
torment rises." It doesn't say that they were **burning** endlessly!

⁶ and if by turning the cities of Sodom and Gomorrah to
ashes (2 Peter 2:6 NRSV)

Reflecting on that same scene, Peter tells us that Sodom was turned to ashes—gone! And yet Abraham saw the smoke rising after it had already become ashes! Rising smoke doesn't mean that a thing is still burning! Sodom was gone! And the rising smoke was simply a memory of what had happened. Simple.

John drew heavily on Isaiah 34 in this same passage. Note the following similarities:

> **8** For the LORD has a day of vengeance,
> a year of retribution, to uphold Zion's cause.
> **9** *Edom's* streams will be turned into pitch,
> her dust into *burning sulfur*;
> her land will become blazing pitch!
> **10** It will *not be quenched night or day;*
> *its smoke will rise forever.*
> *From generation to generation* it will *lie desolate;*
> *no one* will ever pass through it again. (Isaiah 34:8–10)

Both passages speak about: burning sulphur, day or night, smoke rising forever.

Please note something very important here. As a result of the unquenchable burning sulphur, Edom ends up empty and desolate—nothing left there at all! And yet for all this the smoke rises forever! "Smoke rising" forever is clearly a figure of speech. There is no smoke arising there today in Edom [modern Jordan today] and neither is there fire [eternal fire remember] burning in Sodom today!

But there's more.

> **10** It will *not be quenched night or day*;
> its smoke will rise forever.
> From *generation to generation it will lie desolate;*
> *no one* will ever pass through it again.

> [11] The desert *owl and screech owl will possess it*;
> the great owl and the raven will *nest there*.
> God will stretch out over Edom
> the measuring line of chaos
> and the plumb line of desolation. (Isaiah 34:10–11)

Did you get that? Owls will live and nest in a place that is supposedly experiencing eternal fire and is desolate!

Just as Isaiah is telling us that that God punished Edom for its sins against His people so too John says that God will punish the beast and the nations likewise! In spite of all this powerful rhetoric—the persecuting nations in Isaiah (see my earlier chapters) and Revelation still all end up restored!

My point is this: there is nothing at all in any of this judgment rhetoric to suggest an irreversible state. Edom's "forever rising smoke" is not still rising. Sodom's "eternal fire" is not still burning and the fact is that after the judgment it will be restored!

So there is nothing in the language of the hell texts of Revelation to prove eternal conscious torment or instant annihilation. Both hell texts, as we have previously seen, end up with universal restoration!

Judgments, Plagues and Brimstone

The seven trumpets in chapters 8–11 are referred to as plague–judgments (9:18) but are not to be confused with the seven, last plagues. They trumpets serve as warnings to the lost nations; those that do not have the seal of God (9:4). The lost are described as "those who dwell on the earth" which is a technical phrase used consistently in Revelation to describe the persecutors of God's people.

At the time of the sixth seal, the martyrs of God cry out for justice upon their persecutors: "those who dwell on the earth."

> ¹⁰ And they cried out with a loud voice, saying, "How long, O Lord, holy and true, will You refrain from judging and avenging our blood on *those who dwell on the earth*?"(Revelation 6:10 NASB)

In the following verses they are told to wait until the full number of martyrs joins them. But finally their prayers are answered in the form of the seven trumpet judgments!

> ¹³ Then I looked, and I heard an eagle flying in midheaven, saying with a loud voice, "Woe, woe, woe to *those who dwell on the earth*, because of the remaining blasts of the trumpet of the three angels who are about to sound!" (Revelation 8:13 NASB)

It is clear. The trumpets are warning–judgments from God in response to the prayers of the martyrs upon the lost!

These trumpet–plague judgments include "fire," "smoke," "sulphur," and "torment"—which are also found in connection with the lake of fire in 14:10–11.

> ⁵ And they were not given *authority* to kill them, but to **torment** them *for* five months. ¹⁸ By these three *plagues* a third of mankind was killed—by the **fire** and the **smoke** and the **brimstone** which came out of their mouths. (Revelation 9:18)

Here's the same language in Revelation 14:

> ¹⁰ He shall be tormented with **fire** and **brimstone** in the presence of the holy angels and in the presence of the Lamb.

[11] And the **smoke** of their **torment** ascends forever and ever (Revelation 14:10–11)

Although these trumpet judgments are clearly retributive they are still ultimately restorative in purpose intended to trigger repentance unto salvation.

[20] But the rest of mankind, who were not killed by these plagues still did not *repent* (Revelation 9:20)

So we read of judgment, plagues, smoke, fire, torment—this is very similar to the language used to describe the lake of fire—and yet for all this we still see that repentance unto salvation is in view!

Final Judgment and Salvation

Similarly the final gospel proclamation to the world, which is also aimed at "those who dwell on the earth"—that is the lost, persecuting nations at the time of the mark of the beast—employs judgment as the final trigger and appeal to repentance and salvation.

[6] Then I saw another angel flying in the midst of heaven, having the everlasting gospel to preach to *those who dwell on the earth*—to *every nation*, tribe, tongue, and people—[7] saying with a loud voice, "*Fear* God and *give glory* to Him, for *the hour of His judgment has come* and *worship* Him who made (Revelation 14:6–7)

We need to note here that this judgment–unto–salvation warning takes place just prior to the Mark of the Beast and is described in verses 9–11.

For now just keep in mind that a person demonstrates that they have accepted the Gospel if they "fear God and give glory to him." We will come back to this very important dynamic soon.

What is significant at this point is the fact that Revelation 11 describes this same period of time. Chapter 11 uses identical phrases and images to this chapter.

It also speaks about the beast of Chapters 13–14.

> [7] When they finish their testimony, *the beast that ascends out of the bottomless pit will make war against them, overcome them, and kill them.* (Revelation 11:7–8)
>
> [1] And I saw a *beast rising* ... (Revelation 13:1)
>
> [7] It was granted to him to *make war with the saints and to overcome* them. (Revelation 13:7)

Both chapters speak about the "beast rising," "making war" with God's people and "overcoming them." Here I am postulating that Revelation 11 which describes events of the sixth trumpet takes place at the same time as Revelation 13–14 which talk about the final crisis of earth's history.

If that is the case, then this is what is most significant here. Although no repentance takes place by the beginning of the sixth trumpet, the scene drastically changes by its end where most of the world's population comes to Jesus and this just before the mark of the beast is enforced!

This is a big call to make, so we need to camp here a little.

Revelation speaks about the final persecution of God's people by "those who dwell on the earth."

¹ Then there was given me a measuring rod like a staff; and someone said, "Get up and measure the temple of God and the altar, and those who worship in it.² Leave out the court which is outside the temple and do not measure it, for it has been given to *the nations; and they will tread underfoot the holy city for forty-two months*. ³ And I will grant *authority* to *my two witnesses*, and they will prophesy for *twelve hundred and sixty days*, clothed in sackcloth." (Revelation 11:1–3 NASB)

John speaks about the Temple of God and the people of God who worship in it. He speaks about a time when they will preach the Gospel for 1260 days which is the same period (42 months) that the nations will persecute them.

It seems like the church has been eliminated (11:7–8) and "those who dwell on the earth *will* rejoice over them and celebrate; and they will send gifts to one another, because these two prophets tormented those who dwell on the earth" (Revelation 11:10).

But then the scene dramatically changes. The church is vindicated by God in the sight of their persecutors.

¹¹ But after the three and a half days, the breath of life from God came into them … ¹² And they heard a loud voice from heaven saying to them, "Come up here." Then they went up into heaven in the cloud, and their enemies watched them. ¹³ And in that hour there was a great earthquake, and *a tenth of the city fell; seven thousand* people were killed in the earthquake, and the rest *feared and gave glory to the God of heaven*. (Revelation 11:11–13)

During earth's final crisis the church is proclaiming the Gospel one last time. They warn of impending judgment—the seven last plagues culminating with the lake of fire! The church undergoes severe persecution and just then God intervenes to gloriously vindicate them and validate their message.

A tenth of the "city" falls.

So what happens to the rest—the 90% majority at this time? "The rest **feared God** and **gave glory to the God** of heaven!" What?! But wait a minute! We just read those same phrases in the message of the first angel when the Gospel is preached for the last time to "those who dwell on the earth"! We just saw that a person demonstrated that they had accepted the Gospel by "fearing God and giving him glory"! Now 90% of Babylon does just that!

The Gospel message proclaimed during the time of the sixth trumpet, just prior to the mark of the beast is finally received!

Remember that the purpose of the trumpet plagues was to bring about repentance unto salvation.

No repentance has manifested up till the time of the beginning of the sixth trumpet:

> [20] The rest of mankind who were not killed by these plagues *still* did not repent (Revelation 9:20)

This verse is part of the sixth trumpet which starts in 9:13 and lasts until 11:14. It is a long passage and describes many contrasting events. We read of earth's final crisis and the powers of darkness and light facing off one last time. At the beginning of this trumpet we are told that the nations have still not repented. But as this trumpet judgment continues on the story changes!

It is now towards the end of this trumpet judgment that we read that most of the nations—just prior to the lake of fire—finally repent! The trumpet warnings finally work! The nations—the persecuting powers of the world—fear God and give him glory! Remember that to give glory means to repent: "they did not repent so as to give to Him glory"—16:9. To not give glory means to not repent: to give glory means to repent!

Thank you Jesus! Just prior to the end God initiates His first step in His final victory! Ninety per cent of the fallen, persecuting nations end up repenting and accepting Jesus!

This means that only 10% of the nations remain. Regardless of the actual number or percentage, it's clear that these are the very last, the only ones who stubbornly refuse the Gospel and will experience the seven last plagues and lake of fire!

Let's pick up the story during the time of the seven last plagues.

The seven plagues are called the last ones and are part of God's final manifestation of (restoring) wrath.

> I saw in heaven another great and marvelous sign: seven
> angels with the *seven last plagues*—last, because with them
> *God's wrath is completed.* (Revelation 15:1)

We are told that the plagues belong to Babylon. But remember only "ten percent" (the stubborn resistors) of Babylon now remains (18:2,4).

> Then I heard a loud voice from the temple saying to the
> seven angels, "Go, pour out the seven bowls of God's wrath
> on the earth." (Revelation 16:1)

So the seven last plagues are clearly identified as part of God's wrath. Who receives these plagues?

² The first angel went and poured out his bowl on the land, and ugly, festering sores broke out on the people who had the mark of the beast and worshiped its image. (Revelation 16:2)

So it's only those with the mark of the beast—those in Babylon that receive these plagues!

Note what these plagues are called:

⁷ And I heard the altar respond:

"Yes, Lord God Almighty,
true and just are your *judgments*." (Revelation 16:7)

It is during one of the plagues that a heavenly being declares that His plagues are true and just. The plagues are in fact called judgments! You will remember that the final gospel proclamation to those about to receive the mark of the beast included a warning of final judgment! Here it is! This final act of judgment includes the seven last plagues.

Are they purely retributively damning? Is it all over? Is it too late to repent at this time? Has the door of mercy closed forever?

⁸ The fourth angel poured out his bowl on the sun, and the sun was allowed to scorch people with fire. ⁹ They were seared by the intense heat and they cursed the name of God, who had control over these plagues, but they refused to repent and glorify him. (Revelation 16:8–9)

Even now—just like the trumpet judgment—the plagues are designed to trigger repentance unto salvation but the remaining nations refuse to glorify God—instead they curse him!

But it is not over! To be sure, they now enter into the lake of fire but even now it is not the end.

No! God is after the remaining ten percent of rebellious persecuting humanity! The Gospel will win the day—even if it's the final day!

After earth's final crisis we read that the saints—after the mark of the beast—sing a song of victory that includes the future salvation of the persecuting nations who were currently in the lake of fire!

> ² And I saw what looked like a sea of glass glowing with fire and, standing beside the sea, those who had been victorious over the beast and its image and over the number of its name. They held harps given them by God ³ and sang the song of God's servant Moses and of the Lamb:
>
> "Great and marvelous are your deeds,
> Lord God Almighty.
> Just and true are your ways,
> King of the nations.
> ⁴ Who will not fear you, Lord,
> and bring glory to your name?
> For you alone are holy.
> All nations will come
> and worship before you,
> for your righteous acts have been revealed."
> (Revelation 15:2–4)

The saints are now standing beside the "sea of fire" [lake of fire?!!!]

God is referred to as the "King of the nations"! Yes, God is still the King of those in the lake of fire! This is not the end! Why? They proclaim with certainty the fact that the nations at some future time will "fear God, give him glory and worship Him"! Yes! The nations currently in the lake of fire will join the loyal saints in worship as they accept the Gospel message: they will respond to its call as outlined in 14:6–7!

God wins. Love really does win! Not one missing!

Conclusion. The lake of fire imagery employs the exact same terminology and functions as the rest of the judgment language in the book of Revelation. It functions as a climax to all that has been said so far. And God's saving–judgments culminate in victory as the nations finally enter into the city from outside the gates and joins in with the bride to worship the God of heaven—they are finally healed (21:21–27 cf. 22:1–5).

My Thoughts on Retribution in Revelation

I admit that John uses retributive language right throughout his book.

> **6** for they have shed the blood of your holy people and your prophets, and you have given them blood to drink as they deserve."
>
> **7** And I heard the altar respond: "Yes, Lord God Almighty, ***true and just are your judgments***." (Revelation 16:6–7)

We are told that God's plague–judgments are "just and true" in that the persecutors now drink blood just as they have shed the blood of those they have persecuted! This is what they "deserve": this is retribution pure and simple!

And yet these retributive judgments have a restorative end:

> **Just and true** are your ways,
> King of the nations.
> **4** Who will not fear you, Lord,
> and bring glory to your name?

For you alone are holy.
**All nations will come
and worship before you** (Revelation 15:2–4)

Again we read of God's "just and true" judgments which are "deserved" and therefore retributive but they end up with people accepting the Gospel.

How do I reconcile retributive justice with eventual restoration?

As we take in the unfolding storyline of Revelation as a whole we notice an important principle. The persecuted people of God have been killed by the nations and they feel to some extent neglected by God.

> [9] When the Lamb broke the fifth seal, I saw underneath the altar *the souls of those who had been slain* because of the word of God, and because of the testimony which they had maintained; [10] and they cried out with a loud voice, saying, *"How long*, O Lord, holy and true, *will You refrain from judging and avenging our blood* on *those who dwell on the earth*?" (Revelation 6:9–10 NASB)

God's people feel as if God has neglected the supreme price they have paid for their faithfulness to God and to His word. They call for God to "avenge" them by judging the nations —"those who dwell on the earth." He tells them to wait.

> [11] And there was given to each of them a white robe; and they were told that they should rest for a little while longer, until *the number of* their fellow servants and their brethren who were to be killed even as they had been, would be completed also. (Revelation 6:11 NASB)

"Vengeance" would eventually arrive only when the final number of martyrs is complete.

As we read through the unfolding story we see that this "vengeance" by God serves two purposes. We have already seen a number of times now that God's judgments eventually result in salvation for the nations. But before this something else happens.

How can the nations live in harmony in the New Jerusalem with those they have previously persecuted and killed? Things need to be resolved in a final way.

I believe that the persecutors need to understand at an experiential heart level what it is that they have done to the saints. Consider this:

> [4] I heard another voice from heaven, saying, "Come out of her, my people, so that you will not participate in her sins and *receive of her plagues*; [5] for her sins have piled up as high as heaven, and *God has remembered* her iniquities. [6] *Pay her back even as she has paid* (Revelation 18:4–7 NASB)

What has God remembered that He has paid back through the plagues? We have seen a number of times now that the nations persecute and kill the saints (See also 11:1–3, 7–10). How can the persecuting nations fully understand the pain that the martyrs have experienced? The nations experience what they delivered! They experience the same pain they inflicted so that they can feel at a heart level the pain they caused the martyrs. They feel the pain from the perspective of those they had hurt. And I believe this empathic experience triggers their repentance and they turn to God in godly sorrow. In the lake of fire they experience the pain and suffering they have caused, they repent, they wash in the blood of the lamb, and they exit the lake of fire to meet the bride who is beckoning them to enter into the city through the gates.

As they enter the city gates they approach the bride. They embrace and healing takes place, as "the leaves of the trees are for the healing of the nations" (22:1–5).

Can you imagine some of the conversations taking place as they enter the New Jerusalem and meet those that they had previously killed? "I am sooo sorry. I have felt the pain I have caused you. I am sooo sorry." The bride and the nations embrace. The leaves heal the hearts of the nations.

> Then he showed me a river of the water of life, clear as crystal, coming from the throne of God and of the Lamb, [2] in the middle of its street. On either side of the river was the tree of life… and the leaves of the tree were for the **healing of the nations.** [3] There will no longer be any curse; and the throne of God and of the Lamb will be in it, and His bond-servants will serve Him; [4] they will see His face, and His name *will be* on their foreheads… [5] and they will reign forever and ever. [6] And he said to me, "These words are faithful and true" … (Revelation 22:1–6 NASB)

God's ways are faithful and true. Evil and sin are finally dealt with in a climactic way. Relationships between God's kids are eventually restored. The nations finally make their pilgrimage to the Temple to worship with the people of God. The covenant with Abraham to "bless all nations" through the Seed is fulfilled. Eden is restored: the earth is now filled. Together the nations worship their God; they see His face and they reign forever and ever.

And they all lived …

Santo Calarco

S anto Calarco is married and has two daughters. He currently lives in Sidney, Australia.

A pastor and teacher since 1981, Santo attended Avondale College/Andrews University – Class of 1984 and has an MA in Behavioral Science. An avid learner and researcher who has participated in educational studies at both the Graduate and Post Graduate academic levels, Santo is also trained in and has taught Cognitive Behavioral Psychology in Australia. Santo has been involved in Catholic, Protestant, Evangelical and Charismatic Christianity throughout his life and brings his life experience to his work.

In 2019, in recognition for 40 years of ministry; teaching, preaching, writing and healing through the power of prayer, Santo was awarded a Doctor of Divinity by the American Seminary in Houston, Texas.

In addition to his teaching and public speaking ministry, Santo is the sole provider for 770 orphans in Bushbuckridge, South Africa;

supports Free to Dream in their work to end human trafficking; prays for and brings healing to the sick, with numerous documented healings; regularly visits and ministers in Indonesia, bringing hope, healing and financial support to the most desperate and destitute in Jakarta; and conducts a lively and fiery online ministry.

Got questions, comments, perspectives? Santo would love to hear from you!

Email: santocalarco@mail.com

Mailing Address: PO Box 230 Macarthur Square, 2560 Australia

Visit www.restorationforall.com, sign up for his email list, and and get involved with provocative, daily discussions on the Father's love for humanity and the Universal Salvation provided through Jesus Christ.

Made in the USA
Middletown, DE
09 September 2019